Finding my Voice

Finding my Voice

My Journey through
Grief to Grace—
Living with the Loss
of Don LaFontaine

Nita Whitaker LaFontaine
Foreword by Michael Bublé

Finding My Voice:

My Journey Through Grief to Grace—Living with the Loss of Don LaFontaine

2013 Second Edition

2012 First Printing

© 2013 Nita Whitaker LaFontaine

First Edition ISBN-13: 978-0-985-26482-6

Fifth Anniversary Edition ISBN-13: 978-0-9852648-3-3

Information on the butterfly totem is from "Butterfly, Power Animal, Symbol of Change, The Soul, Creativity, Freedom, Joy and Colour" available by Ina Woolcott at http://www.shamanicjourney.com/article/5991/butterfly-power-animal-symbol-of-change-the-soul-creativity-freedom-joy-and-colour.

Use permitted courtesy of Jim Freeheart to reproduce *Angel on the Beach*. www.jimfreeheart.com

Library of Congress Control Number: 2012936537

Jacket and interior design: Sara Dismukes, cusp-studio.com

Published by NitWhit, Incorporated, with Swift Ink Books

This book is dedicated to my beautiful daughters, Skye and Liisi, whose faces and love have been the buoy in the storm of losing their Dad. They have pulled me from the ledge and have also driven me to it, but I have no greater joy in life than being their mommy. The gift they are makes me want to be my best self for them; they've taught me a much deeper meaning of love, and they are the best decision Don and I ever made. They make my life richer, fuller, and sweeter. Thank you my sweet baby girls.

Don will be my muse and I continue to see him in them; that is another gift.

To my mommy, Ola Mae, in her heavenly place and my wonderful Daddy Green, thank you for your amazing example.

Sounds, sounds all around us—the chirping of the birds,
the driving of a nail by the hammer's head, the dull hum of the tires
moving across asphalt and pavement as the motor revs to move it along.
The sound of passing laughter or a half-caught conversation;
a rubber shoe sole on a concrete sidewalk, a distant baby's cry,
the passing sound of music from a moving car or the whistle of a soft wind,
all remind us of life moving all around us affirming and agreeing
that life, like these ever-present sounds in varying volumes, keeps moving,
rolling, humming, crying, screaming, singing, and roaring along.
It is in these moments we know we must join the band.

—*Nita Whitaker LaFontaine*

Contents

5 Years

It's been said that people come into our lives for a reason, bringing something
we must learn and we are led to those that help us most to grow.

—Wicked

Donnie was that for me.

Five years. How can it be? The fifth anniversary of Don's passing feels both foreign and familiar. Getting through the series of firsts, shepherding our children, managing to reclaim my life and new normal all have felt daunting, yet knowing that I'm on the other side of many of them is in a strange way powerful. Once I could get through the emotion of those moments in hindsight was empowering. The lonely nights, his birthday (still the hardest day for me), our anniversary (2013 would be our twenty-fifth), still pull on the deepest longings and saddest strings of my heartbeat. But on top of that agony is the amazing blessing of having been loved like that and to have loved in return.

The other day I decided the files in my office needed purging. In making the decision between "chuck," "recycle," and "keep" I discovered an envelope of cards that I had saved. Funny, I hadn't remembered saving them, but in the bunch of meaningful birthday cards and handmade Mother's Day cards from my children, I found some gems from Donnie. I opened a card and read it, warmed by déjà vu. He finished one card with, "Nita, if my love for you were a song, God would compose it, the angels would sing it and David Foster would produce it!" Yes, I was loved, honored, and treasured, which fills me with tremendous gratitude. Maya Angelou says "Love is liberating, it doesn't bind or hold—it is freeing." I believe that to be true because Donnie taught me that, and showed me its truth every day.

Now, in 2013 and moving toward that September anniversary, I am stronger, wiser, and more peaceful—singing solo once again and liking the sound of my own voice. The difference for me between that first year and now is this warm, knowing comfort of having Don as our guardian angel. I really know that he is. That doesn't change the missing him, the innumerable loving memories that soothe my spirit, or how much I see him in the mannerisms and faces of our daughters. I now walk in the light of grace for having known him. I continue to find my voice as I weather this life storm. But his love still shimmers and rains over all who knew him and those whose lives he touched with his kindness and generosity. My children rush to the aid of their peers who are going through loss; they want to share what they've learned with them. It is lovely to see them emulate their father's caring and giving spirit.

At times it feels like I lost Donnie twenty years ago, and other days it feels like yesterday. In another card I found, Don wrote, "Our children are living, breathing proof of our profound love." They are the greatest blessing of my life and the family bond between us is stronger and more beautiful than ever. And with that I am free— free to carry on with life as he would want us to. Free to laugh out loud and take new risks. I am not bound by grief but instead I use it as an example of what love looks like even as we continue to journey through it. I am learning to play again.

Love frees me to be me and I use the love between Donnie and me as a bridge leading to the next chapter in my life. I will always feel grateful for having known and loved Donnie.

Stephen Schwartz wrote some beautiful words in one of my favorite Broadway shows. In the play, these words are spoken between dear friends as their lives take different paths:

"So much of me is made of what I learned from you, you'll be with me like a handprint on my heart."

Donnie's love liberated me and I always feel his presence—in my heart, in my life, and in the faces of our children.

Foreword

My life has improved through my friendship with Don LaFontaine and Nita Whitaker LaFontaine, and it means a lot to me to be included in *Finding My Voice*. This book is a testament to both Nita's spirituality and to the deep love that she and Don shared.

The first time I met them was at a charity event that music mogul and producer David Foster had invited me to attend. I was nervous, insecure, and—I think safe to say, with no record deal and only change in my pocket—on the outside looking in. Earlier that day I had gone to a rehearsal for a concert that David was musically directing for attendees later that night. I stood in awe as I watched some of the world's biggest stars going through their musical numbers.

I watched an incredibly beautiful woman walk onto the stage (she was striking). When she opened her mouth to sing I was blown away instantly. I turned to one of David's assistants to ask who this remarkable woman was. With a smile he said her name was Nita Whitaker. Even more remarkable to me was how humble, warm, and kind Nita was when I was introduced to her moments later—she simply glowed. She is the kind of person who walks into a room and lights it up. This woman was, well, wow . . . perfect. Mary Poppins perfect. I wondered what man might be lucky enough to call her his own. Two minutes later I found out.

Don LaFontaine walked into the room and everyone immediately felt his presence. Though his charm and charisma were off the charts and he was dressed immaculately, I was overtaken by his rich, deep voice, but also surprised by how gentle he was with it.

At the event later that evening, both Don and Nita noticed my nervousness and took it upon themselves to make me feel welcome and more at ease. I feel lucky to have met them then, and even more fortunate to have continued my relationship with them over the years as they have invited me into their home and into their lives.

When I found out Don had passed I was devastated . . . devastated for his children, devastated for Nita, and devastated for anyone who had the privilege to know him. He was a good man and we lost both a huge talent and an irreplaceable friend when we said goodbye to Don LaFontaine.

I can't imagine what it would feel like to lose my voice, just as I can't imagine the depth of sadness that Nita and the kids felt losing Don. What I really can't imagine is having Nita's courage and fortitude to show us her journey through these past years. Her strength is an inspiration to all of us and her story tells us that with faith and love we will overcome any challenges that we face, even in the darkest of times.

Michael Bublé

Acknowledgments

Starting this journey began for me when I went raw and wounded by grief to a writing workshop led by Jackie Parker. She gently drew out my stories and told me they were "too rich to keep." I was inspired by her words—and those of many in my close circle—to share what I was learning. Jackie gave me the confidence and guidance to begin. You cheered for me all the way. Later, I was led to another light-being angel who would help me bring this book to readers. She has a lilting laugh and a gentle nature and a tad of a Southern drawl; we connected instantly. That person is my new dear friend, editor and project manager, Jessica Swift of Swift Ink Editorial. Truly she has helped me birth this baby. Your tutelage and further guidance have been essential to shaving the rough edges and helping me to focus my story of love, and to walking me through the process. You've been so amazing, quick, smart, funny. And thank you for connecting me with your brilliant book designer Sara Dismukes who added her lovely design touch that made the book feel whole and real. This book would not be a book without each of you. Thank you.

There are so many people who have stood by us in this storm of life. My dad, Green Whitaker Sr., continues to show me faith in action. He so lives in the assuredness of his faith that he inspires me daily. My immediate family, Kathy Scott, Alene Bryce, Green Jr., Aunt Lillian Whitaker, and Dr. Lee Whitaker were there every step of the way through the darkest early moments. You gave so much of your heart, your time, and yourselves to make sure the girls and I were on the road with big backpacks of love from you all.

Paul Pape: my Donnie was your best friend and your relationship stood thirty years. The two of you played off each other's sarcasm and silliness, coupled with years of poker games and Scrabble contests. You made my boy laugh and he, you, and you were standing beside me in the ending moments.

My closest brothers and friends of my heart, Charles Randolph Wright and Adam (Aeyjay) Jackson Jr. (and family) have been loving supports for me and the girls with Adam checking on us every single day and Charles showing up and staying with us when he visited. You were Don's great friends and brothers. You have been there for the girls when they needed a father-figure to impart some wisdom or just to watch over them. What a great support for the three of us since Donnie's been gone. Deb Gates and Johnnie Stewart: you covered me with your prayers when my voice was gone.

I want to acknowledge and thank the kind folks that took the time to read what the book was about and give their sincere comments. It means so much to have your votes of confidence and insights for the book going forward; that this book resonated with you helps me know it will find its place in the hearts of others. Michael Buble', one of America's favorite voices, thank you for writing the foreword and blessing the book. To Josh Groban, you are as stellar a young man as your voice is mellifluous; thank you. Pastor Larry, Nancy, Mark, Wink, Margaret, David, and Ben, I thank each and every one of you for the gift of your words to the book and the honor you give to the love Don and I shared. May your lives continue to be richly blessed.

Don's doctors who became his friends over the years: Dr. Asher Kimchi and Dr. Leslie Stricke, both from Cedars-Sinai hospital, you gentlemen are stellar physicians and cared for Don beyond the call of duty. Asher, you visited Don as a friend, not as a doctor . . . just to sit and talk, which meant so much to us. And to Dr. Heather Jones who fought valiantly with us in those last nine days to keep Don here with us, you are brilliant, kind, and loving.

Jeff Hill and Maria Herrera who have been with my family for thirteen-plus years, helping to make lunches, helping drive kids to appointments, helping me keep the house clean and in order, and running countless errands—you are an extension of our family. It helped so much that we had two loving and trustworthy people in the day-to-day trenches with us.

Pastor Larry Keene: your gentle guidance from the moment we met to the day we laid Don to rest has been a great source of strength for me. You married us, baptized our children and Don, then followed with the ultimate gift of speaking his eulogy in a way that was incredibly uplifting though we felt so heavy. Your wisdom, kindness, and Divine understanding have helped my family and me throughout the years. Thank you, too, Virginia.

My beautiful daughters Skye and Liisi: you are my proudest works, my biggest blessings, and the best decision Don and I ever made. You both illuminate my life. And Christine, bonus daughter, I learned a lot from your growth. To Don's agents, Steve Tisherman and Vanessa Gilbert; for the friends that came with food, banners, time, and love, there are not words large enough to express how humble I feel and how blessed we've been to be in such a village of prayer warriors that held us up, championed us forward, and cherish Don as much as we do. Thank you, thank you, and thank you!

Introduction

My parents told me that before words were clear in my three-year-old vocabulary, I sang. Just threw my head back and made "ahh" sounds on pitch with whatever was on the car radio, in church, or in the community "old one hundreds," where the whole rural Louisiana church would join in and sing call-and-response. I sang before I can remember, and for all my forty-plus years since—I've been blessed in all that time to never once lose my voice. Despite colds and swollen vocal chords, I could still produce some singing sound without great effort.

Nineteen years before I found my voice, there was a little curly haired boy in a sleepy Midwestern town who memorized encyclopedias and could come out of a movie quoting its lines and even singing some of the songs. At age thirteen and only four eleven, his voice suddenly changed mid-sentence into a deep, authoritative tone. And for more than forty years, that voice never failed him. Through more than five thousand movie trailers, hundreds of thousands of tags, and TV and radio spots, he never lost his voice.

That voice almost seemed like a given. Even throughout radiation and chemotherapy, his voice continued announcing five days a week. Even after medicines, illness, and, finally, death silenced him, Don's voice continued to reverberate around the world. Only after he was physically voiceless, did I, too—literally and figuratively—lose my own voice.

In an effort to find my voice again after Don died I began sending emails to a close group of friends. Writing these emails evolved into a way through the darkness of the grief of losing Don and moved me into the grace of having known him. There were so many things that happened that my children did not witness and I could not articulate, though I believe they understood how much their Dad and I loved each other. This book was written to share with them and you the insights, love, laughter, and loss of one of Hollywood's most influential voices: Don LaFontaine. *Finding My*

Voice tells the story of our romantic journey and of two different voices that became one in life and love.

I never intended to write a book—especially one so raw and personal—but I had many inspirations that put me on this road. The first was a quote I heard: "When you tell your story, you can heal yourself and heal others." That is my biggest hope for this book. The other motivation came from one of my favorite teachers, Larry Moss, who said in a class: "The more personally you tell a story, the more universal it becomes." If that is true then I know this story will touch any of you who have experienced any loss.

Though I've enjoyed writing some poetry and songs for my album projects, that was the extent of that creative arm, but I always wanted to get better at writing. I thought Donnie would write a book; he was such a prolific reader, I believed there was a book in him. He wrote a screenplay called *Sandman* that we filmed, but the book never came. I bought him countless leather bound books with empty pages for him to fill, but he always put them aside, saying he just enjoyed reading books and did not want to write one.

When I first started writing my "check-in" emails, which included stories about Don, many encouraged me, especially Pastor Larry and dear friend Neva saying that I should share these stories; that they may help some others walking the road to grief to healing. As I began to tell my stories of various events and memories made with Don and the girls, my coach Jackie said to me, "These are too rich to keep." With that and encouragement from friends and family, and a published article, it occurred to me that I was the one left to share our story. I was inspired along the way not only by the constant support of our family and friends, but also by reading some enlightened spiritual books that helped illuminate the crooked and narrow path during the painful first year, after the crowds had gone and we were left to be a family, minus one.

After Don died, I was moving around in my new normal, trying to be present for my grieving children and myself. Later, when my eldest daughter had gone away to college and my high school-aged daughter was still with me, I found myself with time on my hands that I'd never before had in my married life and life as a mother. I needed a creative outlet. When I received an email invitation to a "Writing to Heal" workshop class in my neighborhood on a weekday night, I thought it could be that outlet.

I quickly discovered I couldn't wait to get to class and began to write some of the stories of my life and love based on random prompts from my wonderful teacher and mentor, Jackie Parker. It was a neutral place and I could write, release, laugh, and cry. I found it cathartic and learned from the other students that we all use different voices to tell our stories.

This book is the journey of how Donnie and I discovered our voices and how that ultimately led us to Los Angeles to discover each other. Ours is a beautiful, rich, love story punctuated by life's highs and lows. We each had pivotal moments that shaped our souls and crafted within us a deeper spirit and purpose. It is a story of black and white—peach and brown love that shone like the sun on the sea and lit us from within. Engraved on our wedding rings was our proclamation that we were One Voice united by a precious, real love and family. The bleak raw road that took us to the door of death when he ascended and the road that I have walked with my children is one that I hope can inspire and encourage others that may be on or will walk this road at some point in their journeys.

Elizabeth Lesser says, "I am fascinated by what it takes to stay awake in difficult times—how we resist, how we surrender, how we stay stuck and how we grow."

I have grown. I have surrendered. I have found my own voice in a world without Don's.

These are our stories, the moments that created our journey to each other, and the love that sustained us to the end and continues to sustain me today, even as I walk my path without Don.

I know he's there.

I hear him all the time.

Long before Don started thinking about his own mortality, he wrote the eulogy for his favorite Aunt Gladys. His words are as poignant and relevant today as they were then, and are a perfect start to my story of journeying through grief to grace.

MAY 25, 1982

Don writes . . .

It happens more and more often as we grow older-

Gatherings like this.

The time of remembering.

Remembering somehow justifies the deep sense of loss –

The helplessness we feel in the face of the inevitability of death.

The words that are spoken at times like these are almost as ancient as the process of passing over, itself. The most eloquent among us becomes tongue-tied, trapped in shopworn clichés and phrases that—no matter how heartfelt and true—ring hollow. Expressions filled with emotion are somehow empty of meaning.

We find ourselves regretting the fact that we put off until another day, the good things—The thoughtful things—The loving things we wanted to do for the one who is no longer with us.

We want desperately to turn back the clock. To live, just one more time—the happy moments, and to replay the bad times—this time with a happy ending.

But of course, we can't alter the patterns of the past. We can't go back to the first square and start over. The moments that have gone, that chances that have passed—have passed, and can never be regained. And so, we are left with remembering. And ultimately, that's good. Perhaps that's all we are left with because that's all that matters, in the long run. Each of us, in our turn, will become the centerpiece of a gathering such as this. The reason for ritual. The rational for remembering.

Remember all the great—and all the little insignificant things that made up their life and all the tender contact points where their life touched yours.

For me, as it is for everybody else, I suppose, it is a totally personal thing—

Secret and sacred—

To be held in the warmest and most private rooms of our hearts.

It's fitting enough that we feel the sorrow—

The sense of loss—

And ultimately, the joy for her or him,

Because they have moved on to another higher plane. She's not gone. She's just gone ahead.

We will meet again. God love you.

—Don LaFontaine

Chapter 1

WAKE UP EVERYBODY

"Wake up everybody no more sleeping in bed."

—Teddy Pendergrass

I was jolted out of my sleep early on the morning of August 22, 2008, by my husband's voice calling, "Nita! Nita!"

I dashed down the hall from the guest room where I'd spent the night with fourteen-year-old Liisi, who was battling a bad stomach flu.

When I got to our room, Don was sitting on his side of the bed, his back to the door. He turned to look at me, his lips blue, eyes wide with fright. Even with the nasal cannula feeding him oxygen, it was clear Don was in trouble. I moved closer to him, heard his labored, rattling breathing, and saw that his nail beds were blue.

"Honey, you're in respiratory distress; I have to call someone." The trained nurse in me went into action as I fought to keep back my fear. I turned the oxygen up to its maximum (five liters), held Don's head against my body, and rubbed his back in an effort to calm him. *If he panics, he might die,* I thought.

"Don't call 911. They'll take me to that crappy-ass hospital," he said, his normally booming voice gravelly and shaky, his whole body trembling. I helped him lie back on the pillows. His breathing slowed as he began to calm down. After I checked his blood pressure and pulse, I called his pulmonologist and got the number of a private ambulance service to take him to Cedars-Sinai where his doctors and all of his medical records were.

He looked up at me with his blue, blue eyes and quipped, "I guess I'll be spending all day in bed."

That's Donnie.

On January 22, 2008, seven months before that horrible morning, I walked into my kitchen to find my invincible husband leaning against the counter with news that would shake the foundation of our lives. In twenty years of marriage, I had never seen Don show fear. This man would have torn apart a bear with his bare hands for me and our daughters Christine, Skye, and Liisi, then bellowed, "Come on, what else ya' got?" But on his face that afternoon was the same look I'd seen when he learned his best friend, Steve Susskind, had been killed in a car accident: shock and disbelief.

"Where are the girls?" he asked.

"Upstairs. Why?"

Then Don said the word that had been lurking within both of us for the past two months. Through the bouts of shortness of breath; the fatigue and coughing; the questionable spot on his colon found in a routine colonoscopy; the collapsed lung that threatened his rich, booming baritone; the bronchoscopy about which the physician had said, "We don't see any cancer,"; and the PET scans. Now, just back from a second consultation with an oncologist, Don said, "They found lung cancer."

I went to him and held him, furious that the doctor had given my boy this bad diagnosis while he was alone. "Whatever it is, we're gonna get through it," I said. The nurse in me knew this was a condition without a cure, but with so many new drugs, his sheer will to fight, and our faith, I knew that we were going to try to beat the odds. *This is my husband, after all—the strongest, kindest man I've ever known,* I thought.

Don had faced other health and life challenges, and he'd looked them in the eye and conquered them. We had a saying when challenges arose: "Well at least it's not cancer. Everything else we can handle!" Now cancer was in the living room of our lives, and we were forced to reckon with the awful fear that comes with just saying the word. Still, I knew Don to be a bull of a man—a tenacious spirit who could rise above anything—and that was what we were going to call upon.

We held onto each other in the middle of our kitchen, and I felt him lean into me. I was the one who usually leaned on him. For a few quiet moments we comforted each other without saying a word. And then we prayed, asking for strength to bear whatever this was. I knew God would see us through.

Don went to his computer to escape. (He loved emailing and watching Rachel Maddow and Keith Olberman. He loved their intelligence.) Though it's my nature to try and fix everything and everybody, I understood. This was one that needed some space.

I called my sister Kathy, my prayer partner, and told her what we had just learned. Calling out to her, I used my voice to gain support and to rally those who would eventually become my prayer warriors throughout our entire ordeal. She was first on my list. Then I broke down and cried.

Kathy fortified me with her faith, conviction, and a word of prayer. She and Don were very close. The fear the word "cancer" brought up in me was overwhelming, and I had to release it so my husband would see only safety in my eyes.

After I spoke with Kathy, I called my two dearest friends, Deb and Adam. They both prayed with me for our family right there, and as they prayed I cried and found my strength and resolve to jump in the ring with this thing called cancer and fight like hell. When I got it together, I did what every woman with a family does: I began to make dinner.

"We will tell people when we are on the other side of this," Don said later. He didn't want anything to get out that could stop his career, so we chose to be careful about who we shared this information with. Don was very old-school Hollywood in this way: it was very important to him that he continue working.

Then we had to decide how to broach this with each of the girls. We called Christine in Florida, Don's beloved daughter—who I call my bonus daughter. She had just had her first child, Riley; a little boy who filled Don's heart with joy.

Christine broke down and cried when we told her. Don reassured her he would be fine—that he was going to kick this thing.

Earlier that afternoon, Don had called home from the doctor's office and blurted out his diagnosis as soon as (he thought) I answered the phone.

"Oh. Do you know Heath Ledger died today, Dad?" eighteen-year-old Skye responded. It was only then that Don realized he was not talking to me and apologized profusely.

When I asked Skye that night how she felt having heard her father had cancer, she didn't seem upset. "Well, Dad's gonna get over it. He's very strong, Mom. We've just gotta fight it."

This is her way, I thought. But Liisi could not have been more different. She is highly sensitive, her emotions often overwhelm her, and at that time she was experiencing enormous fears of death. We made a decision based on what she could handle. We didn't give her the word "cancer", we told her Dad had an abnormality in his lung and he needed radiation and chemical treatment. She accepted our words.

We'd known Johnnie Stewart—a spiritual mentor—for several years, and I had called on her to pray with me many times. I consulted her again in January when there was still so much uncertainty, yet we finally knew what we were fighting. During our conversation she encouraged me to speak positive words with Don. After we talked, she emailed me an affirmation to say with Don. An affirmation is a group of words said repeatedly to facilitate bringing to reality what you speak. It's a vehicle to help you use your voice to bring about change. I wasn't sure how Don would take it, but when I read it to him he liked the idea right away. "Let's do it," he said.

There is a scripture in the Bible that reads: "Whatsoever things are righteous, good and beautiful. Think on these things." (Philippians 4:8) The affirmation Johnnie gave us was very simple and in keeping with this teaching of focusing on all that is good. We focused on the best—on seeing Don healed—not the worst. "I see me well," Don would say to me. "I see you well," I'd reply. Then we'd touch hands to complete our intention.

The girls saw us saying this to each other frequently, but since Don and I had so many little idioms between us they would just shake their heads and smile at each other. Still, on what we started calling "dip days," when Don's energy flagged after chemo, Skye would go into our room if Don was resting, fluff his pillows, and bring him a cup of tea.

Two days after Don's diagnosis, he began chemotherapy. The plan was for Don to receive four cycles spaced three weeks apart, and thirty-five radiation treatments with weekends off. He experienced few side effects.

I located a physician who specialized in a newer area of treatment called integrative oncology. Dr. Mary Hardy had an office at UCLA and was a New Orleans native, in my home state. Before our first visit, she'd read Don's entire medical record. Within two seconds of meeting us, she "got" Don, gave him a strict low-food chain diet, and prescribed several herbs and homeopathic remedies to balance out the effects of the chemicals he was receiving.

Through the seven weeks of treatment, the oncology doctors at Cedars kept telling us what an amazing patient Don was and how well he had done with this aggressive treatment (combining chemotherapy and radiation). With his usual upbeat attitude and steady stream of witty comments and jokes, Don kept everyone at the hospital laughing. No matter the situation, Don would find some way to ease any tension with a quip or a good-hearted tease. He quickly traded insults with the doctors and nurses, commenting on everything from their "sensible shoes" to calling someone on a fart. He in no way behaved like the King of Hollywood that he was.

The Geico commercial Don appeared in made him recognizable after twenty years of relative anonymity. In it, a woman says something and Don, wearing earphones, repeats her words in his highly dramatic "voice-over" voice.

"In a world where both of our cars are totally underwater," he intoned in his famous announcer's voice. "In a world" is a phrase familiar to millions of moviegoers—one Don created more than thirty-five years ago, when he was a writer and editor in the movie trailer business. He'd voiced it in thousands of movie trailers from *The Godfather* to *Fatal Attraction; Shrek* and *The Simpsons,* and it's been parodied by comedians from Pablo Francisco to Janeane Garofolo. But Don never made a big deal of it. Don was the same in the hospital as he was in our living room.

Off-the-wall humor was just part of life in our household. Skye and Liisi grew up with a Dad whose daily comments put us all in stitches. It wasn't unusual for them to see me drop to the living room floor rolling with laughter. Don would think nothing of dancing into a room with a new hip-hop routine (at which he was awful), playing it for the laugh. At bedtime, he'd make up stories to tell the girls, including hilarious character voices that made them both squeal with delight.

I admit to bursting into song at all kinds of inappropriate moments, like belting out "You can't touch this" by MC Hammer (complete with the dance) for no apparent reason. Sometimes I made my daughters sing for their supper—literally, no song, no food. Some mornings, I'd be boogying them off to school and as the garage door closed in front me I'd hear Don call out, "Look at your wonderful mommy," as he smiled with pride.

And throughout treatment Don kept his life as normal as possible. He continued to drive the morning carpool: Skye two days a week, Liisi one. He always pulled energy from somewhere when his children were concerned. When he returned home we would get back in the car, and I'd drive us to Cedars, sometimes listening to Eckert Tolle's *The New Earth*. Don loved what Tolle had to say, but listening to his voice, Don said, was like taking a Nembutal. The drive there and the quick radiation treatment (all of two minutes) would take about an hour. When we got home by late morning, Don headed downstairs to his studio to work.

Don loved his work with a passion, and he wanted to keep doing it as long as he could. But he only wanted to give his best, so on a day when his voice wasn't producing the sound that was up to his standards he would not do a job. Those days were few and far between. "My clients pay me a lot of money for my sound," he'd say, "and I'm not going to put anything but my best out there."

That's Donnie.

Don had a phenomenal career voicing more than five thousand movie trailers. In the year 2000, when the Cannes Film Festival held a tribute to him in France, he experienced for the first time the impact his voice had in the world of movies. As we walked into a huge, flower-decked room filled with eight hundred people, Don turned to me and asked, "Are all these people here for me?"

In addition to movies Don did close to seven hundred fifty thousand TV and radio commercials. And then there was his announcing: everything including CBS News, *Family Guy, America's Most Wanted,* and the 2007 Academy Awards. He'd had many stellar days during our marriage where he'd record twenty-six separate spots in one day. He was known in the business for his capacity to work. And his voice never failed him. Even as he battled cancer, Don was Don through it all. He kept his trademark attitude: "Let's fix this thing and keep it moving. I've got some more living to do!"

A man of impeccable integrity and standards, Don's energy was deep as an ocean and as powerful as his voice. And even facing the biggest challenge of his life, Donnie never flagged. I could hear him say, "Early morning carpool? Chemo? Radiation? What else ya' got!?" His faith and motivation spurred him on to maintain a sense of normalcy in his life.

That was Donnie.

In a world where love rules, Don LaFontaine would be immortal.

During Don's treatment we held a true belief that he would fully recover over the seven weeks of radiation and intermittent chemotherapy. And through it all we held fast to our faith, our family, and our love: we continued to be one voice united.

Chapter 2

KISS ME IN THE RAIN

"Kiss me in the rain, make me feel like a child again."

———

—Barbara Streisand

In June, two months after Don's treatments were completed and a mere two months before that fateful day when he woke up gasping for air, we thought we had won. Don's PET scan—a CAT scan with an intravenous iodine dye to highlight any abnormalities—looked clean despite a lot of lung swelling. We felt we had beaten it—and the odds. We prayed, praised God, and celebrated with tears of joy. Later we learned Don's doctors believed they had only a twenty-five percent chance of eradicating the cancer. We considered the clean scan the miracle we all prayed for. Little did we know this terrific high would be short-lived.

Even though the radiation treatments were completed in March, chemotherapy continued until early April because it is given only once every three to four weeks. At one time, Don's blood count was too low and he couldn't receive chemo until he was given a blood transfusion. Once his prescribed number of treatments were fulfilled, we traveled to New York to celebrate and see a couple of plays; we had close friends in two Broadway shows and wanted to support them. Don had been a New Yorker for twenty years and I think he wanted to go there as a special trip for the two of us. He wasn't a hundred percent yet but we went anyway, taking some portable oxygen in case he needed it. It was great not being tethered five days a week to the hospital, and to have chemo treatments behind him.

But at the end of May, Don's labored breathing returned. Tests showed this was just a normal side effect of his treatment, a condition called pnuemonitis: inflammation of the lung. Don was prescribed steroids to decrease the swelling.

A month later, when he showed no improvement, the dosage was increased. Then came more side effects, including tachycardia (accelerated heart rate) and steroid-induced diabetes. We were not deterred; we believed if we could get the dosage of steroids right, get the inflammation down, and balance his diabetes.

Through it all, Don stayed strong and looked well, continuing to work as much as he could. But by early August, even climbing the eighteen stairs from his studio became difficult. Then he landed in the hospital.

When Don arrived at the Cedars emergency room on August 22, he was awake and alert, but with a blood oxygen level dangerously below normal. The private ambulance I called had arrived with two female paramedics to take Don to the ER. They had a heck of a time because their gurney didn't fold and they couldn't carry him down eighteen steps to the front door. Suffice it to say it was quite an ordeal; each time they tried to lift my two hundred-pound boy by wrapping their arms around his chest, it would throw him into breathing distress that oxygen couldn't seem to soothe. We needed man power and all we had was estrogen.

Once they were on the way, I checked on Liisi, who had fallen asleep in my closet exhausted from her stomach flu and lack of sleep. Once I had both girls settled and Skye watching over her little sister, I drove as quickly as I could to be with Don at Cedars. When I got to the ER he was already looking and feeling much better. His color was pink and his nail beds and lips were a normal color. After trying several combinations of oxygen masks and different levels of oxygen, the ER doctor placed a Bi-Pap mask on him, giving him a steady, pressurized level of oxygen to maintain his level in the range they wanted and he needed.

"This Bi-Pap just bought Don a bed in ICU," said the attending physician. I was grateful, knowing he'd get highly personal care there.

"You should go to rehearsal now," Don said, "I'm fine."

I put my hand on my hip, rolled my neck, and said in my best southern black-girl attitude, "Have you lost your mind? I am not going anywhere!"

Under the Bi-Pap, he smiled.

I was four rehearsals away from opening in a five-show run of the musical *Once on This Island* at the UCLA Freud Theatre and had just started accepting a few out of town gigs again. The week before, I'd gone to Omaha to sing as the special surprise guest at a private birthday celebration. Don was my greatest fan; he was always so proud of my work and wanted me to be performing. And here he was on a bed in the ER with pressurized air being forced into his lungs, worrying that I would miss a day's rehearsal. It was so Donnie.

When I called the director and explained why I wouldn't be there he said, "Take as much time as you need, we understand; this is your husband."

The ER nurses stabilized Don—they got his vital signs within a normal range so he was able to breathe without working as hard, and his color was good—in about forty-five minutes, which was about the time I arrived. Everyone was moving with urgency and intention. I was impressed with their highly effective teamwork and felt good that Don was at Cedars and in such capable hands. Since his medical records were already there, he had been spared having to give his history from scratch—and the last thing you want to do when you can't breathe is talk.

Though the oxygen helped, it still was not clear what was causing Don's pulmonary distress. Even though the Bi-Pap restored his oxygenation to a somewhat normal level, in order to discover what had caused this incident the attending physician ordered a CAT scan. We waited and waited, but they were so busy that by late afternoon it wasn't done. Around three o'clock they finally had a bed for Don and I was told they would take him for a scan on the way there and it would take about an hour and a half to get him settled. I decided to run home and check on the girls, though I'd been giving them updates on and off. While driving home, the head doctor from the ICU called to give me the names of the doctors who were going to be in charge of Don's care and reassured me they were some of the best lung specialists in the country.

Once I arrived home Don called—speaking right through his Bi-Pap mask—asking me to wait until after eight to come back to the hospital. The nurses would be changing shifts, he explained, and I wouldn't be able to get into the ICU until then.

Through his mask he said hello to "Bug and Buglet," his pet names for the girls. They were happy to hear his voice. Skye had been sitting beside her father that morning, comforting him when the paramedics arrived. Liisi had been asleep and blessedly missed seeing her father struggling for air.

Earlier, I'd called Don's closest friends to let them know he was back at Cedars, and when I returned that night Paul Pape and our pastor, Dr. Larry Keene, were in the ICU room with him, the three of them having a lively time, laughing and talking as if they were sitting around our living room.

After they left, Don and I hung out in that clean, square little ICU room with only the heart monitor going and one IV line in place, just in case meds needed to be administered quickly. He was awake very tired, though still talking away. He was not considered critical anymore but he was not out of the woods yet.

"I guess this is where I will spend my birthday," Don said matter-of-factly. His birthday was four days away.

The year 2008 had been a year of hospitalizations for Don, most of them short, including two others during the summer. I knew he was beginning to get frustrated. He wanted the steroids to work so he could get back to his life. I reminded him about those short stays and told him this would be a short one, too. And I believed it. Then we talked about how we'd be going to Dubai soon—Dubai being Don's next dream destination.

We both loved travel—it was our gift to ourselves—and we felt blessed to be able to give our girls the perspective of seeing other cultures. Don was a history buff, insatiably curious, and with a computer, a microphone, and an internet connection, he could travel and record spots at the same time. "Might as well pay for the trip!" he'd say as the girls and I went off on a short outing while he stayed in the hotel room or stateroom to record a series of spots.

In July 2007 we went to Spain on a cruise, and then to Scotland. There we'd stayed in an eight hundred-year-old castle on magnificently manicured, sprawling grounds. At each historic structure, Don would bend down to touch the lowest stone; "The one first laid by the hand of a man."

In 2005, we traveled to Italy and Greece. In the sweltering heat, Don knelt to touch the lowest stone of the Parthenon. He was in heaven on this trip at the temple of Olympian Zeus; the Vatican in Rome; the *David* in Florence; the ruins of Pompeii; and the canals and glass blowing in Venice. It was a dream trip for us all, and we took it in with gusto, thrilled that the girls were able to see these amazing places. Our childhoods had been nothing like this. I'd glance over at him on that trip and see his face lit with little-boy delight.

Though we talked about our travel plans, by ten thirty Don was urging me to go home. He'd been in the hospital since ten that morning, and he was concerned the girls were alone. I didn't want to leave him. He'd asked the nurse earlier if he could have something for sleep. He was exhausted, having slept only a few hours the past six nights. The nurse explained that a sedative might compromise his breathing. He was going to have to try to sleep without medication. I worried that he would not have an easy night. Before I left I leaned over and nuzzled his cheek, lifted his oxygen mask, and kissed him on the mouth, and we said I love you's. I got up reluctantly.

Then, just before leaving the room I paused at the glass door, looked back at my husband, raised my hand and we spoke our affirmation.

"I see you well," I said.

Don responded, "I see me well."

Chapter 3

HIS EYE IS ON THE SPARROW

"His eye is on the sparrow, and I know He watches me."

—Hymn

It always blesses me to sing, and for as long as I can remember there was singing all around me. My father was a local gospel soloist and president of the church choir. As a toddler, the youngest of the four Whitaker children, I would sit on my Uncle Leroy's green linoleum floor in a house just across the backyard from ours in Shreveport, Louisiana, looking up at my handsome, six foot three daddy, Green Whitaker, practicing with his group, The Spiritual Jubilee, seven men who seemed tall as giants to me. They sang without instruments, just the patting of the foot and the rhythmic slapping of the hip to keep time. The harmony was five-part, with my dad usually singing the top notes in a contra tenor voice, and the other men filling in the tones to the bass notes. It was infectious, heartfelt, and delightful to my ears. Secretly, I thought of them as my own singing giants, and on Friday or Saturday nights, as they practiced at Uncle LeRoy's or at our home, I'd be down on the floor singing right along with them, following every part.

I'm told I was three when I sang my first solo in church. One Sunday I was lifted onto the offering table of Mary Evergreen Baptist Church in a little rural town called Frierson in my crisp yellow dress, long skinny legs, white lace socks folded just above the ankles, and shiny patent leather shoes. When I sang "Yes, Jesus Loves Me"—chorus and verse—my father, a strong southern gentleman, broke down in tears.

I remember many Sundays standing buried in the congregation at Mary Evergreen, my head thrown back, singing hymns and "Old One Hundreds," the call and response songs whose words I didn't understand. Right beside me stood my beautiful mother, Ola Mae, my sisters, Kathy and Alene, and my brother Junior, in our washed and starched Sunday best. Around us were chocolate, Sunday-hatted women fanning themselves in the Louisiana heat, the sound of the plank floor knocking as a hundred heels tapped them in the rhythm of the songs. All those voices collected in a hollow sacred space became harmony that will always stay— and resonate—with me.

As a small child, I'd sing for anyone. I had never learned to be afraid of performing. Green and Ola Mae taught me that my voice was a gift from God, and even as a rotten-toothed five year old, whenever I was complimented on my voice I would say what I had been told. I believed it with all my heart.

Soon my sisters Kathy and Alene, my cousin Debbie, and I formed our own singing group. We called ourselves—with such originality—The Whitaker Sisters. Whenever Daddy's group sang, we'd be the bonus treat.

"I got a surprise for y'all," he'd drawl to the congregation, "My babies gonna sang for ya'!"

We performed in small churches in the Ark-La-Tex (Arkansas, Louisiana, and Texas area), at least two Sundays a month. Even at five, I was pushed to the front to do the lead, my sisters and Debbie behind me, for "Do You have an Account in the Bank in the Sky?" an old Clark Sisters song. Alene played piano—often out of tune and sounding like something in a saloon.

At the end of the service, The Spiritual Jubilee would receive a "love offering": a little bit of what had been given in the basket.

At the ripe age of six, I was invited to sing at my favorite cousin Red's church (his real name was Booker T. Whitaker, but none of us called him that), where he played the organ. Red could make that organ talk, as we like to say in the South.

It was a big and beautiful charismatic church, three hours away in Dallas, and I'd never experienced The Holy Spirit take hold like it did that day at Cousin Red's congregation.

My parents drove Kathy, Debbie, and me to Dallas where the three of us would stay for the week with Cousin Red, his pretty wife, Jewel, and their baby boy, Kenon. Cousin Red and his little family lived in a beautiful stone home in a very nice section of town. It looked like a mansion to me: hardwood floor, paved streets with sidewalks, and three or four bedrooms.

My dad and mom taught me two songs that I would sing for solos. One was "I Trust in God" and the other, "He'll Understand."

When Sunday morning came, we piled into Cousin Red's car and drove to his church. I sat in a middle pew next to my sister and Cousin Debbie and watched the service begin, with the black-robed deacons leading hymns and saying a prayer. I had no idea when I was going to be called up to sing, but Cousin Red had given me a signal: when it was time, he would point at me from the organ. The services continued and no signal came. It felt like an eternity of waiting. Suddenly Cousin Red was pointing to me and mouthing, "You're gonna be next." My heart sped up and I took a deep breath. I wanted to sing good for these Dallas people and make my cousin proud.

After the offering Cousin Red stood up at the organ and said, "We have a fine little singer that's come to us today all the way from Shreveport. She's my first cousin, and no offense Kathy an' ya'll, but she's my favorite."

Then I walked up from the congregation to the organ and stood at a microphone that was adjusted for my height. Cousin Red played the introduction, and I began to sing "He'll Understand." I was singing real well and was into the second verse: "Misunderstood / The Savior of sinners," when all of a sudden a lady in a middle pew stood up and shouted, "Glory! Glory!" and began to dance. Soon she was jumping wildly in the aisle, and it looked like people were trying to restrain her. Now, I had seen shouting before because folks in my home church shouted too.

I closed my eyes and tried not to focus on the lady and go on with my song. Then I got to the part that says: "Oh hear Him call / His Father up in Heaven / It's not my will but let Thine be done" when a man jumped up and started bucking like a horse—like he was having convulsions. All of a sudden he fell like a board, straight back onto the floor.

My six-year-old self was terrified by what was happening to these people, and I could feel tears taking hold. I tried to keep going—that's what my daddy did when people shouted as he sang—but the tears stopped somewhere in my vocal chords and made the sound come out croaky. I kept on trying, croaking out those words, tears running down my face, until a lady came up and put her arms around me and escorted me to my seat. She gave me a Kleenex, Cousin Debbie patted me on the back, but Cousin Red just kept on playing that organ—playing the notes like he was singing them.

I couldn't stop crying. I was scared to death and so embarrassed that I hadn't finished my song. Everybody around me was whipped into a frenzy, and all over the church folks were shouting, "JESUS," and "Yes, Lord!" The place was on fire! It was something to see, and it didn't hit me until later, at Cousin Red's home, that my song had moved these people to dance with the Holy Ghost. Glory! I learned the true power of singing that day.

Nineteen years earlier and a thousand miles away in Duluth, Minnesota, in a world before television, a little boy named Donald LeRoi LaFontaine also discovered the power of his voice. At five, Don sang soprano in the choir at a Lutheran church in northwest Duluth. At home, he listened, transfixed, to the old time radio story hours and the great singers of the '40s. With his perfect pitch and uncanny memory for lyrics he sang right along with his favorites, Bing Crosby, Frank Sinatra, and all the crooners of the day.

The boy soprano knew some cold winters and hilly walks to school, but even in kindergarten, Don's voice was loud enough to be heard over the voices of the other children. His teacher was not amused. "Donald would make all the noise he wants to, if he possibly could, though his ability to sing is unusual and his pitch excellent," wrote Miss Maxine C. Thoorsell of Lester Park Elementary on Don's kindergarten report card. She described the five-year-old Don as "a vivid personality, strong willed. He would usurp all the attention and use all the kindergarten material if he could."

The boy soprano's larger-than-life personality was quite the challenge for poor Miss Thoorsell, who believed Donald suffered from having been given too much attention. Though she tried using a firm hand, it was no use. Don the entertainer was born. He soon learned to spice up each school day with a little slapstick comedy, endearing himself to his classmates—if not his teachers—throughout elementary school.

When he was ten, Don learned to dance the Lindy Hop. He and his younger sister, Sandra, practiced it in the long hours when their mother, Rubie, was at work. Rubie was a single mother—a rarity in the 1940s—who worked first as a waitress and then later on the assembly line at Western Electric. Her struggle to support her two children instilled a strong work ethic in Don and Sandy. Still, she showered them with as much love and attention as she could. Meanwhile, Don and his sister soon became such a great Lindy team they started entering local dance competitions—and winning.

All through school, Don continued to excel at being class clown, but it was the sudden deepening of his voice that gave Don a real sense of what vocal power could do. At thirteen, Don's voice changed in the middle of a sentence. He didn't go through the awkward voice cracking phase most pubescent boys experience. It just suddenly dropped.

One evening as he was helping his mother do the dishes, Rubie remarked that Don was unusually silent and asked why he wasn't talking. "What is it you want me to say, Mother?" Don replied in his new baritone voice. With that he was sent to his room for being sassy.

This deep booming voice coming from a five-foot-tall frame had some decided advantages. He could sound like anyone's dad calling from the office to get a student out of class. He could call in sick for the student who wanted to ditch school. In eighth grade, Don became wildly popular with this new talent—and something else happened. He could suddenly get girls. The ability to convince through the power of his voice and the ability to attract women—these gifts were Don's by the age of thirteen, two attributes that would come in very handy as an adult.

After years of practice using his voice to woo women, Don and I met. Don appeared to be quite the playboy, a man as far from the ideal as anyone from my good-girl church-going background could have been. But as we grew in love together, the playboy fell away, and the man stepped forth to meet me. And we learned that even coming from such different backgrounds we had much in common, including the gift of our voices that had sent us on our paths into the world and each other's lives. We were soul mates, without a doubt. Race hardly entered into it, except in the beginning when I wondered what an older, rich white guy like Don, who could have any woman (and often did), would want from a five-foot-ten-inch country girl like me.

In the beginning I held the line, and our friendship came first. And by the time Don started saying, "I like the concept of you," I found myself—against my better judgment—falling in love. It was a romantic and challenging two years before we married. By the time we did, we knew we had found our home in each other.

For our wedding in 1988 the photographer asked us to give him a big batch of childhood photographs so he could create a montage that would be shown at the reception. We had a pile of pictures from our early years ready to go and Don thought out loud, "How is he going to tell us apart?"

"Don, really?" I said. "I'm black."

"Oh—oh, right." And we collapsed in laughter and love.

I thought of our two decades of marriage, our work and family, and our challenges and joys, as I drove to the hospital to see Don on his second day he was there. Yet even under these conditions I was looking forward to the hours I would spend with him. There was no moment with Don that I did not look forward to. I knew myself to be blessed, despite these awful circumstances and the terror we faced on this late August day.

I had just picked up my usual chai soy latte at Starbucks and was back in the car, about fifteen minutes away from Cedars, when my phone rang and an unfamiliar voice said, "Hello, this is Dr. Heather Jones. Is this Anita LaFontaine?"

I recognized the name of the lung specialist I had been told about the day before. "Yes, this is she. What's going on?"

"Are you driving?" she asked. "I want you to be safe." Her voice was warm and full of concern.

I knew a bomb was about to be dropped.

"I can pull over," I said, though I had no intention of stopping.

"At about six this morning your husband got really sick. We've had to intubate and sedate him. I need your permission to give him blood. He isn't able to consent."

My heart started racing, the thump-thumps so strong it felt like it was going to explode out of my body, but the nurse in me answered automatically. "You can type and cross-match him. How many units?"

"I think for now, just one."

I told her I would be at the hospital shortly. I called my best friend, Adam and our pastor and told them Don was very sick, then drove into the parking structure, my mind racing. I headed toward the ICU without a clue as to the enormity of what I was walking into.

Dr. Heather Jones had been so calm when we spoke on the phone about giving Don blood. When I left him the previous night we were talking and planning for Dubai, but suddenly Don's condition was critical. I was buzzed into the ICU and walked down the hallway with its curtain-covered glass-fronted rooms, some with patients in them, some empty.

As I approached the fifth room I could see Don, but I couldn't believe what my eyes were showing me. It looked like he was surrounded by octopi, there were so many IV lines going into his body.

He was on a ventilator, and from his terrible stillness it was clear he was heavily sedated, in a deep, deep sleep. There was a tube in his mouth, his limbs were at odd angles that reminded me eerily of a yoga position—the suvasuna—legs at forty-five degrees, arms at thirty. Around him were doctors and nurses, a flurry of activity. I stepped into the room and Dr. Heather Jones, longhaired and blonde who looked like she could be one of my girlfriends, was at the head of the bed getting ready to perform some kind of procedure. White sterile paper covered Don's neck and shoulder. She looked up and gave me a smile and gently said, "Do you mind waiting outside. We're still working on him." I felt like all the wind had been sucked out of me. My legs went weak, but I did what I was asked. They were trying to save Don's life.

This is not happening. This is not real, I thought. *It must be some mistake.* I left the room, stood a few minutes then found myself walking back down the hall past the nurses' station through the electronic doors. In the waiting area I saw my friend Adam coming toward me and I fell into his arms. Deep, gut-wrenching cries came through me from a place inside myself I did not know. I felt as though my voice was caught in this guttural sound. A primal, animal instinct to make some noise in mourning even when no words were possible in me. In this moment I saw my voice starting to fail.

Chapter 4

TIGHTROPE

"Whether you're high or low you gotta tip on the tightrope / I can't complain about it, I gotta keep my balance and just keep dancing on it."

———————————

—Janelle Monet

Don's condition remained critical. Having been on the other side of this unfolding drama as a nurse, what I saw with my professional eye looked quite ominous. After I gathered myself, I asked Adam to make some calls on my behalf and I phoned my sister Kathy, who had only just left the Wednesday before. When I tried to speak, only sobs came out. She simply said, "I'm on my way."

I called our bonus daughter Christine who had been busy planning her wedding to Riley's father; she was stunned by the news and began making her plans to come.

Each time I had to repeat to someone that Don was in critical condition and on a respirator, it became harder and harder to say. I couldn't believe it myself. *Might I awake from this fitful dream at any moment to find it to be nothing more than a terrible nightmare?* I wondered.

Only when I was finally able to walk into his room, after they placed a large needle near the base of his neck called a CVP line, and saw the constant care needed did I realize we had not only opened, but we were inside, Pandora's box. Once allowed back into his room, I was able to fully assess the gravity of the situation though there was still a shock factor. Many things were going on and there was a lot to take in as I looked at my gravely sick husband fighting for his life. It was more than overwhelming.

No less than eight IVs hung, each with a different bag or bottle of some sort of clean solution medicines hoping to slow down or undo the ripple effect now going on. He looked like a medical experiment in a lab; his naked body lay beneath stark lights with people in scrub suits quietly scurrying about. Doctors spoke in hushed tones. He was sedated and appeared unconscious, but I know from my time in nursing that the patient can always hear you. Having already cried, I was aware Don would sense if I spoke with dread in my voice. We knew each other so well and our voices were so often the first indicator for each of us that something was amiss.

I leaned in over the beige handrail of the sterile bed and the starched white sheets and placed my cheek upon his and said, "I'm here honey. You got really sick and they're trying to figure out why. I know you can hear me and I won't leave you. I'm here." He tried to talk to me and he began to buck the ventilator and move one of his arms.

Because his lungs were so taxed from the adult respiratory distress and he had been a long time asthma patient, trying to respond to my presence caused him more stress; his oxygen levels dramatically dropped, or he de-saturated (in medical terminology) and he certainly did not need that. Doctors increased the sedative. I comforted him and tried to calm him with my touch, with light singing, and reassuring him with my voice.

I cannot recall who came into the room next but there was a constant flurry of doctors and nurses. He had to be placed on dialysis because the meds that helped increase his blood pressure also temporarily shut down his kidneys. I could not leave his side; there was so much going on and I needed to know everything. The nurses and doctors were very understanding and efficient but it was all too much—a sensory overload of the heart. I felt like I was in somebody else's nightmare.

I occasionally would have to step out for this or that procedure, or when they tried to do a CAT scan. At those times I'd leave the ICU and go around the corner to a waiting room that filled up with loved ones coming to support us over the course of the day. Adam and Paul had already arrived, and my family arrived late on August 23—my two sisters (my brother couldn't be there), my father, and my sweet Aunt Lillian (my mother's best friend and sister). Don loved her very much and she had been a surrogate grandmother to our girls, often staying with them when we traveled. Each time I saw someone new, I wept at the kindness of their presence.

Our girls were sleeping in on that Saturday morning and I eventually had to call them. I sent a friend over to our home to be with them. I told them what I could over the phone; that Daddy had become very, very sick and that I needed to be with him at the hospital. My sweet Liisi was so afraid and Skye grew quiet. Later that evening a college girlfriend picked them up and brought them to me. I met them in the parking lot. My youngest watched me walk toward her, reading my body language. My older daughter trusted me to tell her the truth. That was as much as they could handle.

Our angels continued to arrive; people were spilling over with outrageous acts of kindness. People showed up with flowers, food, blankets and snacks, or they simply sat and held my hand, prayed, picked up my children . . . things I didn't ask for that they just did. Just seeing them gave me the strength and fortitude that I needed. Their eyes, hugs, and sad hearts were my shot in the arm and short adrenaline trip back to the boxing ring to fight alongside my daughters' sweet father.

Never in my life have I experienced such a symphony of love from so many. My sisters slept in chairs in the waiting room that night. I stayed in Don's room with the pings, the whoosh and low rumble of the air mattress beneath him, the swish-gasp of the respirator, and chirping of IV machines. I had to be with him. I kept saying throughout the night, "I'm here, Donnie," and I'd rub his feet, or kiss his face and hands.

The doctors repeatedly said they were trying to balance everything; to get the meds just right without giving him too much. The ventilator was set to its maximum capacity to ensure his body had the proper oxygenation. His heart rate was strong and steady and his blood pressure was being shored up by various medications. Myriad other meds—antibiotics, blood thinners, insulin, antiviral meds—all danced together on a delicate tightrope of hope in an effort to balance his body in the fight for his life. Hope was all we had in the chaos of it all.

Aunt Lillian went home that evening to stay with the girls. I could see how sick Don was but I also knew how much he wanted to be here for us and with me; I could feel him fighting. The image of him lying there stayed in my head when I tried to go to sleep, and conjured up the time when my mother became gravely ill.

My earliest memory of her was the smell that I've come to know as Estee Lauder Youth Dew. It was an oil-based perfume that stayed with her always even when I went to her bed at night with a sick stomach or a scary dream. She would wake us on cold wet Louisiana winter mornings by turning on the lights, then pulling back the end covers and putting socks on our feet. She'd always say that breakfast was the most important meal and we could not leave without having one prepared by her loving hands. I remember being in the fifth grade in the beige-tiled school bathroom with a friend discussing how I couldn't wait to wear a garter and stockings just like her. (Pantyhose had not happened just yet.)

Mother Ola Mae, my mentor, my muse, was a smart dresser and a savvy shopper. She believed in us girls wearing pretty things to bed so we had lovely nightgowns and jimmies just like she did. She could find a sale rack or an offbeat store and find clothing and shoe gems for her four children (my brother required special shoes that one of my father's jobs paid for) that made us appear to be a wealthy family. She could sure stretch a dollar.

She stood about five foot six with shoulder length black press and curl hair, smooth semi-sweet chocolate skin, white straight brace free teeth brushed only with baking soda, full lips, and a quick warm smile. She had a small waist, warm heart, a beautiful figure, wore a size ten shoe, and had been born the eldest of fifteen children to Lois and James White. She was brought up on a farm and taught to be humble and obedient but her nature was always of kindness, politeness, and an eagerness to help others. I was told that she would go barefoot during a high school class so that her half-sister Jarutha could use her shoes for gym class. She was kindhearted and giving. She and my dad were a perfect match.

After losing their first two babies to late term miscarriages, my brother Junior was born; a six-month preemie, he survived but later would be diagnosed with cerebral palsy (though mild) because of developmental delays. He never learned to crawl. His legs didn't work so well, but he was a happy drooling baby often dressed in white. My mother and dad were so happy to have this baby that she kept her floors clean so he could skooch around on them in his white outfits. They took him everywhere. It wasn't uncommon at this time to keep your disabled child at home or to put him in an institution. Not my brother. He has perfect diction and that was due to the way my parents, especially my mother, mainstreamed him, talked to him, worked with him, and put him in every normal situation possible. I was learning also while she was teaching him. How did she know this was right?

I know what a gift she was because she was thinking ahead and wanted a broader world for us. I believe she followed her keen maternal instincts. Mom was my hero. She and Dad managed to functionally raise four children into productive kind people who are still an intact and loving family today. Where she got the energy, the drive, the perseverance, I'll never fully understand. I do know that I wish to be that kind of beacon for my two daughters. Though I only had Mother for seventeen years, she packed a lifetime of memories into my heart. She was a wise, amazing, and spiritual being; if I can stand in her shoes at any time in my life, I think that would be wonderful for me. I always knew I was loved and cherished. I too know what a blessing that is. This blessed mother taught me about mothering, being a good citizen, and caring for my family. I hope to be just like her. All that I need to know about being a woman in the world, I learned from her. She was a remarkable woman.

I always knew mother was special but as I've become a mother, now I am convinced she was a genius ahead of her time and certainly an earth angel, just like my Donnie. At the end of her life, my mother was on a ventilator and heavily sedated was a memory that I could not shake for years. For a long time I couldn't remember her walking, laughing, or being the Mom that I knew; the only images were of my seventeen-year-old self feeling helpless in the face of what was happening. I chose not to hand the albatross of seeing their father in the exact opposite way of how he lived his life to our young daughters, especially on that tightrope kind of day.

I realize now that even as I thought about my mother's death, I was actually reflecting on her life. I was strengthened by the memory of her and resolved to continue fighting for the life of my precious husband, my angel. I wanted to focus on his life. I thought, *He cannot die today.* Didn't think about the girls being without their father in that moment. I just wanted information and for him to stay alive. That's all. Keeping him here and getting the right balance of drugs and sedation so that he could survive. Not only was his life on the ropes but so were ours and for those first twenty hours, all I could think was, *Don't take him, please . . .*

Chapter 5

SOMEONE TO WATCH OVER ME

"There's a somebody I'm longing to see, I hope that he turns out to be; someone to watch over me."

—Ira Gershwin

We were emotionally charged with our *fighting for his life* boxing gloves on our third day, a Sunday. My bonus daughter Christine flew in from Pennsylvania with her small toddler child, Riley, and then-fiancé, Mike; my father, Green, who loves Don like a son; my sisters Kathy and Alene; and Aunt Lillian. Adam, Paul, and Pastor Larry, all kept constant vigil with me since their arrival Saturday. I could not nor did I want to leave Don's side.

As word got around, the waiting room filled with our close friends and family. Don's Uncle Dick (who was being treated for pancreatic cancer) and Auntie Char drove up from San Diego with their daughter Cheryl. Though we were all distraught, people gathered there to give and gain support and love and at this stunning turn of events for our beloved boy. I don't remember how I told the girls that Daddy had become very sick but I know that I called them; that's all I remember of telling them. It's a blur now but I remember they were not at home; they had gone to friends' houses later that morning when the drama was unfolding. It was a day of receiving friends, spending as much time as possible with Don, retelling what I knew to those who called, staying on top of the meds and the medical tests the doctors were doing, and trying to keep my wits about me.

Even though it had been a long time since I'd been an ICU nurse, instinct kicked in immediately. I needed to know everything and to be spoken to as a colleague and not just as an afraid and overwhelmed wife. Don's primary doctors would come in and out, particularly Dr. Asher Kimchi who had long become Don's friend as well as his cardiologist for nineteen years.

After my sisters arrived, my college girlfriend Pat brought the girls to the parking lot of the hospital later that evening; they were overwhelmed and didn't know what to think or feel except fear and dread. Liisi watched me as I walked toward the car; she and Skye were assessing my body language because they could read my face and tell if they could feel safe. They slowly emerged out of the car and tumbled into my waiting arms. Looking into their puffy eyes, we hugged and kissed for some moments. I gained strength just from holding them. I told them everything I could that I knew to be true at that moment: that Daddy was very, very sick and the doctors were figuring out what had gone awry in his body. I reassured them of how strong Daddy was and what a fighter he was. I also gave them permission not to go into the ICU to see him. Trying to be strong for me, they had gotten most of their crying done before getting to the hospital and were numbed by the news.

They were so fragile and were frightened to see their powerful Dad laying so still that I felt the ICU was a bit much and decided to have them remain outside. I stayed in the parking lot with them for an hour or so and we shared some laughs to lighten the heaviness for a moment. They were ready to go home and I had to entrust them to each other's love and care and the support of my amazing friends who showed up in herds for us.

Later that night, our dear friend Ben Vereen flew in from New York to be with us. Seeing Ben reminded me of the time when Don and I first started dating. Ben hired me for my first professional gig when I moved to Los Angeles as a background vocalist with Don. We rehearsed at Debbie Reynolds's studio for three weeks along with Tony Warren (best friend and awesome singer), Wendy Fraser, and eight musicians. It was a tight, fast-paced show staged by Jaime Rogers. I felt so lucky to have landed a real singing job and not have to go to the hospital for my twelve-hour nursing shifts from seven to seven. Don and I had only been on a couple of dates, but he was very forward in saying that he wanted me to be his girl. I thought he was moving too fast and I told him as much. I was not in the mood for a boyfriend, having recently gotten out of a stinker of a relationship. All I wanted was a singing career. But there he was with those blue eyes . . .

First stop on the tour with Ben was a two-week engagement in Lake Tahoe; we stayed at the Valhalla Inn down a snowy road in Tahoe, and walked uphill to work at Harrah's two shows a night. I did not have a cell phone in 1987 though Don did (quite an expensive toy) so I'd just give him a call from the room to say hello and he would always send flowers wherever I was staying. Such a romantic . . . I loved that about him.

Next stop was Hollywood, Florida, playing the Diplomat Hotel. The band members and singers stayed across the street in another part of the hotel, and we played two shows a night there for another two weeks. I learned so much watching Ben perform show after show; he is a masterful showman, brilliant and legendary. We were there for two weeks and I'd given Don a call on our second night there. It was February, near Valentine's Day, and flowers came. I was thrilled to get them. One day he called my hotel room. I asked where he was thinking he was somewhere in his house. He said, "I'm in the lobby." I thought he was joking; we had only shared a couple of smooches so far, and yet here I was in Florida and he was supposed to be in California.

I said, "What lobby?"

He said, "At the Diplomat."

I reminded him that he lived in Hollywood, California, and I was in Hollywood, Florida.

Then I said, "What are you doing here?"

He simply said, "I was in the neighborhood and I came to see you."

"I'll be right over," I said. I hung up the phone, jumped and danced a little and squealed with delight (at least a high C) in my little hotel room, brushed up my makeup, and did another little dance. Never had any man gone out of his way for me or had any man other than my Dad done something so over the top for me. I wondered what Don's gesture meant. I asked myself, "What does he want from me?" We had only gone on two dates, so you can imagine my shock and delight in the same moment.

He had flown all the way across the country to be with me and to get to know me better. Was he trying to impress me or woo me? I didn't know because I didn't know him so well, but assumed perhaps it was a little of both.

I ran across the street and dashed into the lobby where he stood leaning against a giant post near the lobby entrance wearing a medium blue V-neck sweater that matched and accentuated the blue of his eyes. His dark brown blow-dried hair and mustache added to the Burt Reynolds–like drama set against the dark wash jeans; he was very sure of himself, all five-feet eight-and-a-half-inches of him. He looked six-feet tall to me that day.

I ran to him but didn't want to give the signal that because he'd done this for me, I was supposed to do something for him, so I was cool and didn't fawn over him, but I was really touched.

He came to all the shows that weekend. We spent time together during the day and continued getting to know each other. He had a sweeping suite at another hotel overlooking the ocean, and each night I went back to my dinky room with no view and modest amenities because I did not want to be perceived as an "easy" girl. My standards were too high for even this grand gesture to make me give in to the moment. I wanted his respect more than anything else and I wanted to get to know him better, to see if he was real and if we could really be a couple. I was not giving up the coo-coo!

We took long walks, ate delicious lunches and dinners, and spent lots of time talking. He seemed wonderful and terribly romantic and I was learning that his playboy exterior housed a really gentle man. I could feel that he was growing more special to me by the minute; he had always been clear about his intentions. "I want you to be my lady," he'd said. We were gently reminded that we were in the South, and felt stared at a bit, with my being tall and him shorter, but getting used to that came easy. That time together marked the beginning of something wonderful and significant between us.

I learned later (long after we were married) that Don had gone to Ben to ask his permission to come around and date me. Ben reminded him that he was not my father. Don nodded and acknowledged that he was my employer and he wanted it to be okay for him to come around. He gave Ben an expensive bottle of wine I was told as a gesture of goodwill and gentlemanly behavior. Ben was very impressed with him and ended up being one of two best men at our 1988 wedding. He and Don had tremendous respect for each other's brilliance. They had a quiet friendship based on that respect and mutual love, never judgment or competition.

All of these memories flooded me when the hospital's elevator doors opened at around ten o'clock and I saw Ben. I was really happy to see him, I appreciated his grand gesture of love and kinship, as most of the family was going home at my insistence because there were only chairs to sleep in at the hospital. And I wanted my family home with my girls.

Ben and I sat and talked and laughed between my visits to Don. Ben did not want to go into his room just yet. I made a pallet on the floor to try and get some sleep at around one. I thought Ben was being picked up and I thanked him for coming. When I awoke at six the next morning and as I was headed back into the ICU to check on Don's status, there, sound asleep, hat askew to cover his eyes and propped up in a sitting chair in a most uncomfortable position, was Ben, watching over me. He was that someone to watch over me that night; my angel while I slept for the first time in thirty hours.

Chapter 6

WE ARE A FAMILY

"We are family like a giant tree branching out towards the sky.
We are a family; we are so much more than just you and I.
We are a family growing stronger, growing wiser . . . we need you."

—from *Dreamgirls*

I went home to get a shower forty-eight hours after Don had been admitted to the hospital. Even though I hadn't gotten much sleep, I sent out a mass email asking for prayers.

August 24, 2008

Dear friends and family. I'm reaching out to all of you. My wonderful husband is in critical condition at Cedars-Sinai Hospital; they believe a blood clot is lodged in his lung and he is fighting for his life. This happened on Saturday morning after he'd been taken in for severe shortness of breath on Friday. He was stable and I left him talking and being funny, planning our next vacation. He is very sick right now and we need your concentrated prayers! Have your churches, synagogues, and temples send prayers for Don's healing and wellness. Light a candle, chant, whatever you do to send that loving energy and light to him. I would appreciate it. And save a little for the girls and me. We have had small miracles already and if we all shout up to God collectively, I know how powerful that can be. I am spending most of my time there. He is fighting and we all are fighting with him. He is strong and is a warrior so I thank you in advance for your prayers, good wishes, and kindness on behalf of my family.

With a hopeful heart,

Nita and family

As soon as I got my shower and sent the email, I went right back to the hospital; I didn't want to miss a thing. I was so overwhelmed; I knew that I needed help praying for Don through this challenge—I couldn't do it on my own. Though I had called my close family and friends, we needed the prayers of a vast village, so I reached out with that first email and asked for what we needed.

At one point an attending physician asked me if I wanted to place a DNR (Do Not Resuscitate) on Don's chart. *Is she asking me to give up? Is she saying that he stands no chance for survival? I feared.*

I was incredibly incensed. How could she suggest that a DNR was all there was at this point? My rule at home with the children when an injury or complaint happened was to give it seventy-two hours to see what transpired; we hadn't even reached forty-eight hours yet. I was adamant that this was not the end. This day, no way! And if my boy couldn't fight, I would fight for him and for our family to stay whole and intact. How could she ask me something like that on just the third day of this craziness?

I said to her, "How dare you ask this of me! We have two children and I want to you to do everything in your power to keep him here with us. Do not ask me this on day three!"

She replied calmly, "We are doing everything now."

But I wasn't ready to accept that; I wasn't ready to sign Don's life away nor did I believe that there was nothing left for the doctors to do to save my boy. I walked to the waiting room and fell apart with my family and friends. My heart raced. Sadness and pain welled up like vomit in my throat. I tried to suppress it and made it worse as my heart pounded faster. I wanted to escape the ICU to a place outside the confusion of everything I was feeling. And I didn't want Don to witness me coming undone.

I fell into the arms of my sister with loud sobs that rolled like a stormy sea; when I thought I would stop, I couldn't. My face was wet and ugly from the enormity of the decision the doctor had asked me to make, what she was asking me to let go of. I could not—would not—let go of my Donnie.

After I collected myself and breathed, I went back into Don's sterile room with its humming machines and octopus arm IV lines. Another resident who was also in Don's room mentioned to me that they could give him a medicine called TPA that would dissolve the clot they thought was in his lung. He warned that the side effect was that Don could bleed out anywhere else he had a lesion, like the one in his brain. This was news to me.

"The one in his brain?" I asked.

I knew nothing of this latest brain lesion diagnosis though I had been on top of his care and every medical detail. I asked this young doctor to be sure he was talking about the right patient. He acted as if he were telling me something he thought I knew. I felt emotionally assaulted: first the DNR question and now a brain tumor?

My brain was inundated with so many questions: How did I not know this? Did the doctor make a mistake? Did I miss something? Did Don not tell me, or was I not informed? With so much going on I didn't know what to think. Then I got angry, or shall I just say pissed? All I knew was that I wanted my husband back the way he was. I didn't want any of this. It felt like I was ripped out of my life and placed in an episode of *Grey's Anatomy*. Everything felt heightened and out of sync. Doctors huddled around trying to understand the underlying illness that caused Don's catastrophic downturn; waiting for Dr. House to come, as the mystery spiraled. The scene mirrored a sci-fi flick where everything is grossly enlarged but the voices are low and garbled. It was an out-of-body-experience as things swirled around us like Dorothy from *The Wizard of Oz* when she is caught in the eye of the storm.

The doctors put forth their best efforts to determine exactly what had occurred in Don's body but that did little to help the anguish I felt as we all tried to grasp and understand what we were up against.

My sister Alene walked with me into the waiting room filled with loved ones, where I repeated what had been said to me about Don's brain lesion. Then I fell apart again. Soft sobs came in waves this time, and my body swayed with them. I was spent, but simply couldn't stop crying. It had all been too much. I cried for the seven months we'd just survived, from the fear I'd locked away, for having to possibly tell my girls more bad news—and I wept for myself.

I sat with that information for about two hours while I waited for that young resident to come and tell me something—anything—different. When he didn't I finally resumed my hourly visits to Don's side where I saw him.

"Have you checked your information?" I asked.

"Oh I'm sorry, it was the wrong patient," he said casually.

I wanted to slap him but I was too weary to do it. It was an emotional roller coaster and I could not keep it together. I prayed and cried until I had no more tears.

Then, for the first time in my life, I lost my voice. Too worn to even speak, I knew this was the beginning of a life that would never go back to what it was. Don had always been my bulldog boy, my pillar of strength. I suddenly felt like someone pushed my mute button and silenced my voice. The day's dread, weariness, and overwhelming moments zapped the life and sound from me.

I needed to hear Don's booming baritone. I wanted to be soothed by his voice, to gain comfort from his velvety tones, to see his earnest blue eyes reassuring me that everything was going to be okay. His voice was the part of him that I was attracted to: his perfect diction and low, enveloping rumble-tones always made me feel comforted and safe. If Don said it, I believed it. Often I would ask him to repeat something just because his voice made me feel warm and safe and I'd kiss him for saying it again. His voice had been in perfect harmony with mine for more than twenty years, and right now neither of us could make a sound.

As I sat in my quiet, my body shook with each thud of my heart which I could hear, slow and thundering within me. I cried enough water to fill the River Nile with my tears. The only sound I could produce then was that of an exhausted baby who's cried hard—each breath is punctuated by a series of mini-aspirations. In many ways, I felt like a baby.

Each hour I would go into Don's room for forty-five minutes to be near him; to hold his hand, to sing to him, or to give him a daily bath and rub his feet. These gestures were all I could do for him other than stay on top of all the medicines and treatments they were giving him and monitoring his daily test results. Listening, watching, and praying became my daily routine. In my past, I'd been the nurse on the other side of a situation like this, administering the meds, comforting the family, being available to answer questions with great empathy. Now I was the one who needed comfort and explanations. I felt weird and misplaced. The emotions are so very different when your loved one is laying in a hospital bed hanging on to his life.

Don's vitals always improved when I was in the room though they had to keep him heavily sedated. When they didn't, he would try to pull out the endotracheal tube that connected him to the respirator. I know he was trying to say, "What the hell is happening here? Get this thing out of my throat!"

I grew concerned about that tube because it was passing through his amazing vocal chords so he could not speak to me though I knew he wanted to. I couldn't hear his voice and be comforted by it.

All the while, there was so much havoc and upheaval in the teetering tightrope-walk to hold on to life. I didn't want our daughters to have the image of their father in that bed in that way. Don always showed them his strength. Even when he didn't feel great, he would puff up for the girls. I knew in my spirit that he would not want them to see him in that state. I made that decision after prayer and speaking with my father and my pastor. I kept them informed of the daily goings-on and I told them how sick Daddy was. It was the most awful of days trying to find a medium in the swirl of events that surrounded his existence with the devastation that was; it seemed we hung in the air with his life in the balance.

There were many new doctor faces, some residents, some on call, coming in and out this third day—all with specific duties covering Don's care; a team per se. Some were infectious disease doctors, some were kidney specialists, others were internal medicine; they all worked to try to piece together the puzzle of this sudden grave illness. Many challenges presented themselves and I was asked many times to make life decisions on Don's behalf. Faced with having to make the decision not to place a DNR on his chart, or okaying a further life-threatening procedure, I wanted to get it right. But in these vulnerable moments, the last thing I was able to be was a clear thinker.

Around four o'clock that afternoon, the day centered on determining the root of why Don had become so ill. He was maintaining life with help from the ventilator and many meds, but there was a great need to know exactly what happened so they could correctly treat the malady. The doctors, especially Dr. Kimchi—his cardiologist—had a strong indication that it was a pulmonary embolism (a blood clot in the lung), but wanted to confirm the diagnosis with a CAT scan, but this procedure could not be done in his room. At the same time, his fragile body wouldn't make it to the appropriate department without a team of six.

An additional obstacle to moving Donnie was his dangerously low blood pressure; he had been placed on vasopressor meds to raise it. As a side effect, this med shuts down blood flow to the kidneys as a way to provide more blood flow to the vital organs: heart, lung, and brain. This put him into acute renal failure and he was placed on constant dialysis. This is often reversible if the blood pressure begins to normalize, and the vasopressor can be weaned. But at this point, he needed the vasopressor to sustain his life, and yet we were presented with the choice to get the CAT scan, even though the ride down could cause him to die. If we did nothing, I was told he would die.

Dear God! I thought. *I cannot make this decision on my own; it is too big. Please give me guidance.*

I went into Don's room to talk to him. Over the constant low hum-click of the dialysis machine and the intermittent hiss of the ventilator, he lay very still on the hospital bed, sedated and covered by a single white sheet. He looked peaceful, but the IV lines and the way the fluorescent lights lit the sheets and the machine gave him an eerie stillness and gray tint.

I told him that we were fighting for and with him and that we needed him to do as much as he could to fight, too. I told that I loved him and reminded him that I would be there. I told him how much he was adored, relayed messages from loved ones, told him who was here with us and who was on the way. Whenever I left him I told him a little joke, since we so loved laughter.

The totality of this day and the weight of the decision of whether to take him down for the scan brought me to the brink of emotional exhaustion. Through my angst-filled tears, I asked for help from my family and friends who were gathered there.

First, I called my daughters and told them I needed them to come to the hospital because Daddy was very sick and the doctors needed to do a big procedure. One of them asked if Daddy was going to die and I vaguely remember saying I hoped not but we needed to be together. I assumed it would be a long night, so I told them to bring their laptops and a blanket.

My sisters left to get the girls and bring them to the hospital. Around six o'clock I asked the close-knit group present in the waiting room to voice their opinion about what they thought we should do concerning Donnie. I asked them to help me make this decision because I didn't feel I could make it on my own. Some said they believed whatever I thought was best was the way to go. Others felt as though Don would want to know what the culprit was and hopefully give the doctors an accurate chance of treating it.

Then a miraculous thing happened: we began to pray. I don't know who started, but it went around and lit up that waiting room on the fifth floor of the Saperstein Tower at Cedars. The small room surrounded by upholstered chairs, large windows that let in lots of light, clean white walls with a few pictures for color, and blue industrial carpeting—there we sat in two rows, facing each other, and the prayers made the rounds.

A light seemed to fill the place and me; the weight of the moment lifted. The prayers carried me to a calmer place in my own spirit. For however long that was, we were united in a fervent prayer for Don's life to be spared and for him to be given more time, however much that would be. I felt my angels all around me— both in that room and hovering above.

After listening and waiting and praying, I ultimately made the decision I thought Don would have wanted and what he would have made for me if the situation were reversed. The doctors had been blanket-treating him for everything because he was so fragile they couldn't obtain all the data to pinpoint a cause. I decided that we would go for the scan the results from which would provide direction for targeted treatment.

We went into the ICU to tell the doctors our decision, and we were told the scan would have to wait until an hour after the nurses' shift change, which happened between seven and eight o'clock. Only then could they get him ready to roll with all the IVs, dialysis machine, and respirator.

My children arrived at seven forty-five and were greeted with loving arms and hugs. I was much happier having them with me. Just seeing their scared little faces forced me to be stronger. I wanted to shove them back into my womb to protect them from the heartbreak of this day and its unknown outcome. This was real-time—real life, and even though my mother bear sprang up, I couldn't protect them from it.

We waited for the doctors to come and tell us it was time. I was holding my breath, knowing that moment was around the corner. This could be the day we lose him, *the last day I might ever see him,* were just some of my tormented thoughts. But I was also in constant prayer in my mind and spirit that a miracle would come. It sounds like pie-in-the-sky thinking to those who may not believe as I did then and still do now.

I heard the doors open and around the corner came three female doctors who had been on Don's team that day, and they had good news for a change. I remember so vividly what they said to us.

"Don just turned a corner. He began making urine on his own (indicating that his kidneys were beginning to function again and his blood pressure was on the rise). The first order for a doctor is to Do No Harm and so honoring that, we've decided that we will just wait and see how he keeps improving."

The timing couldn't have been more significant; my children thought they were coming to possibly say goodbye to their Daddy, but he had been given a reprieve . . . of sorts.

We all celebrated and blessed the prayers we'd prayed together. Against all odds Donnie miraculously survived that terrible day. Not one of the doctors expected it. I so wanted to know what was going on in Don's mind. I heard his spirit say to me, "I'm not done yet. I'm still here."

Though they cautioned that he was still very ill, I knew without a doubt this turning of the corner was the miracle we'd prayed for today. It wasn't grand like the parting of the Red Sea; still, there is power in the extraordinary miracles of small things, like yellow urine dripping into a bag on the side of a hospital bed. We are a family, built on love, cradled in togetherness, and nurtured by each other's prayers. I realized that day the strength of my collective family.

It's a good thing I believe in angels: I easily recognize them. I know that Don was an angel and so were the friends and families who gathered at the hospital to support me. As I rested in the love of my diverse angel-family, I had no idea how heavily I would I lean on them in the days yet to come.

Chapter 7

ARMS OF THE ANGELS

"You're in the arms of the angels, may you find some comfort here."

———

—Sarah McLachlan

We can see the mystical and the magical, the natural and the unnatural, if we are open to receiving them. As a small girl I was keenly aware of my connection with angels. They were my protectors and just as I know it now, I knew it then. It wasn't paranormal activity in the way portrayed by the movies, but rather a calm unseen and sometimes seen presence that always comforted me. Perhaps because of my rural Baptist upbringing, I've always felt this connection to the Divine.

At age eleven or so, my family and I were driving to Denver, Colorado, to visit cousins of ours. Being the youngest, I sat carefree on the front seat of our 1964 beige Bonneville. The highway stretched as far as I could see on this blue-sky day, and the road seemed endless. It was on this trip that I had a first sighting or vision from some of my angels.

The trip we were on was meant to have included one of my father's brothers, Booker T.; we called him Uncle Book. He'd had a long-suffering battle with prostate cancer, which he'd lost. Both Big Mamma (Daddy's mom) and Uncle Book passed on within a year of each other and I knew that my father felt terrific sadness.

As we drove in the beauty and quiet of that afternoon, I recall gazing up, trying to count the scattered clouds to pass the time, when out from one of those clouds appeared my grandmother and my uncle waving at me with big smiles—Big Mamma adorned in a beautiful white gown that seemed to shimmer, and Uncle Book wearing white, too. From my center seat between my parents, I pointed to them. "There they are! Uncle Book and Big Mamma! They're waving to us! Can't you see them? They're right there!" I said, continuing to point.

My dad, who is a magical, spiritual man, shouted, "Where, baby, where?" as he tried to see them too.

Perhaps they were just for me to see, but he did try. My mom thought I'd awakened from a dream, but I had not been asleep. She quieted me, but I kept looking at my angels, owning what I was seeing and feeling a bit sad that I couldn't share what I was witnessing with anyone else. I knew those angels were watching over us as we traveled and I remember I felt somehow safer.

As early as I can recall—and especially in the loving home my parents cultivated for us—we learned the teachings of Jesus, the presence of angels, and stories from the Bible. My parents were devout Christians and our home strictly held onto those traditions. It was all I knew. That home at 522 East 73rd Street was my castle, my safe place. Though modest by today's standards for me, it was a mansion and I was a princess with royal parents who were firm yet loving. They married with eight dollars between them and created a home and life that grew as our family did.

My sisters and I shared one large room with two closets, a built-in desk for three, and three twin beds. My brother got his own room and the kitchen was the center of our home. It was a home typical of the time, with wall-to-wall carpeting except the kitchen, and paneled walls in the den and lower halves of the hallway.

Mother loved cooking and a splash of the modern. Our kitchen had six high-backed orange chairs that swiveled along a white breakfast nook that ran the length of the L-shaped wall. In the center was a round white table with two more chairs that completed the set. It was a kitchen ahead of its time in our small Cedar Grove community—so named because of the rows of cedars that were there before it was developed into a subdivision with gravel streets lined with houses full of working-class black families. It was the kind of neighborhood where the neighbors watched out for each other's kids, and where we were the dreams of our parents. They wanted a better life for us and they had worked hard to reach a better station than their parents.

My Dad worked five jobs during this period of our lives—two full-time and three part-time—to support the family. He said people criticized him because he worked so hard, but he felt nothing was too much for his family.

Mom was a librarian and worked a forty-hour week on the bookmobile or in the parish library. It is interesting to me now that the man I chose to marry would have so many of the traits my parents possessed: a great love of family, learning, and hard work. Many schools didn't have libraries when I was in elementary school, so the library came to us. Mom was beloved because she was seen as a giver of knowledge. She'd also have the driver take that bookmobile into the rural communities and walked from door to door, handing out books for children to read and often coming home with red dirt on her low-heeled shoes. Even though our community was a middle- to lower working-class neighborhood, I always felt rich. Such comfort was there on 73rd Street. We knew each neighbor and child, and we played ball together in the streets. There in my neighborhood, in a simpler time, summer nights were filled with the symphony of the insects, times spent trying to catch a lightning bug so that we could capture his light, the smells of fish or chicken frying, and legs and arms being slapped in a fight against biting mosquitoes. I remember feeling safe, loved, and surrounded by angels. My parents were earth angels who were simple, kind in thought and deed, and worked to make our home a peaceful, loving place. Green and Ola Mae Whitaker solidly built my foundation of love and faith in that house on 73rd street.

The first time I brought Don home to meet my family we went to visit my favorite Aunt Ginnie's home on 78th street. It was a shotgun house that I knew well since Debbie lived there and we often spent the night at each other's homes. Aunt Ginnie was a great cook like my mother. Although she'd lived with an alcoholic husband, she never complained and always kept her wits and dignity about her.

I was a little concerned about Don being dropped into this all-black world, being the rice in my family's raisin box, but he insisted that he had to meet my Dad because of my love, respect, and adoration for him. My Mr. Hollywood Burt-Reynolds–look-alike complete with the mustache who lived in a slick modern four-level home and drove a car worth more than most of my family's houses, sat with those blue eyes in a living room the size of his bathroom. He didn't care; all we saw was each other. As we sat on the plastic covered sofa in that small living room, my five-year-old cousin Dawn crawled into his lap, looked up with big brown eyes and said to him, "I have a white boyfriend . . ."

Don just smiled and hugged her a little harder, knowing this was a small sign of acceptance. Don fell in love with my whole family, and they fell in love with him. He made them laugh, and they him. He was charmed with their genuineness and salt-of-the-earthiness, and they were impressed by his gentility and warmth.

After we returned from our weekend visit, which included a visit to my old charismatic church with full-on shouting and gospel music (it was a first for my Catholic-raised boy), a nice lunch at a local restaurant, and some time between he and my Dad, I called my Dad and asked what he thought of Don. He told me that he thought he was a good egg but that he "liked the drank a bit much."

I told him, "His heart is so good . . . I'm working on the other."

And with that, I knew my dad in his own way had given me the go-ahead. He saw the heart in the man Don was, and was impressed that he'd gone out of his comfort zone to show me how important I was to him. It would please any father. So with a wink and a nod from my earth-angel Daddy, I was ready to fly with this new relationship into a world of love I couldn't have dreamed.

They say girls marry their fathers and boys marry their mothers. How true that was for me when I came to realize that my Donnie was an earth-angel, just like my dad.

Chapter 8

HAPPY BIRTHDAY TO YOU

"Happy birthday dear Donnie, happy birthday to you!"

Like Don predicted he was indeed still in the hospital on his birthday, August 26—
four days after his arrival. He was holding his own, with small improvements daily.
His blood pressure rose enough that the doctors were able to decrease some of the
meds, there was a little yellow urine in the bag, and he had better blood oxygen
levels.

Prayers and good wishes flooded in from all over the world. People were
dropping by the waiting room and some curious ones tried to get into the ICU
to see him but there were strict rules applied and I was an enforcer along with
my sister. Johnnie called the women who helped me WMDs, Women of Mass
Destruction. They were fiercely protective of Don and me, and they were the
elevator screeners. People we didn't know had to go through them, which was no
small feat.

The usual gang of angels was there daily: Pastor Larry, Paul, Adam, Cousin Dr.
Carl Whitaker, Ben, my father in-law Papa Nick, Uncle Dick, Rachel and my family,
and even more of our friends came to give me a hug, lend support, and join the
vigil. That part of the journey was amazing, and still is to me.

My routine was to go into Don's room every hour to be a part of his care, but
today was his birthday so we planned that during his bath time—which Dad and
Carl wanted to be a part of—we'd sing for him.

Don adored my father and day after day, he would come in and lay his hand on
Donnie's chest and say, "Son, it's me, Pappa," then lean down and kiss him on the
forehead.

Pappa Nick, Don's stepfather (Clifford Nikka), came to sit a while too. He and Don's mother, Rubie, were married forty-nine years and even in 2008 he still reeled from her death in 2004. It was very difficult for him to see his son lying in bed, so helpless. But Donnie gave us great responses when we went in and sang a three-part harmony of *Happy Birthday*.

His oxygen level jumped to 100 percent. His usual level was around 90 to 92 percent. His oxygen level only rose when he could hear me. I know hearing my voice made him want to speak to me, but his heightened oxygen intake also let me know he was happy I was there. It was one of the few ways we communicated through his induced sedation and intubation. It was as though he was showing me he was fighting in the same way he'd puff up at home when the girls came into the room; he couldn't speak now, but his actions did the talking as much as they could. Then, as we gave him his daily sponge bath and body rub, we sang three spirituals in three-part harmony. The nurses came in and out, smiling.

Later that day, I asked Dr. Jones (Don's primary care physician in the ICU) to watch some YouTube videos of Don. She was caring for a heavily sedated patient, but not getting to know the vibrant, larger than life, love of my life.

She burst out laughing, watching "Five Men in a Limo," which Don had written and performed with four other voice-over guys. It was important to me that she get to know the man he was. I needed for her to see his wit, charm, humor, intelligence, and humanity. Often, doctors can only see what is presented to them. I wanted Dr. Heather to get a glimpse of the man I loved: the wonderful, witty, irreverent, hard-working, loving, peaceful, outstanding human being that laid in that bed.

Like all of us, Don's childhood shaped and reinforced the strength he carried his entire life. Born Donald LeRoi LaFontaine, he was the first child of Rubie Virginia and Alfred LaFontaine. He was named after his grandmother, Donalda, and went by Donald for most of his youth. In a small mining town at the tip of Lake Superior, a five-foot five-inch soldier with striking blue eyes, dark brown hair, and a baritone voice would marry blonde, blue-eyed, five-foot two-inch Rubie. Fresh out of a home for girls, she had big boobs, a small waist, and was quite the looker. Their marriage was not to have the fairytale ending to match its beginning, ending in divorce when Don was barely four.

To make the height requirement to get into the military, Alfred had to hang from a tree and be carried lying flat in the back of a truck to stretch his body. Still, you'd want him on your side in a bear fight. Legend has it this short man took down five others who were indecent toward Rubie. Domestic violence wasn't spoken of in those days, but I learned Alfred was insanely jealous and had quite a temper that would often fall on Rubie.

But Rubie was smart enough to get out with most of her teeth and sanity, even though being a single mom in the '40s was tough. Don's sister Sandra was two years younger, and at one point, Rubie found it so difficult to make ends meet that she took them to an orphanage, but she went back to get them the next day because she couldn't stand it. As soon as she was able she got her children back and Don and his little sister Sandra had to fend for themselves while hardworking Rubie labored to keep a roof over their head and to keep them together.

She worked hard as a waitress like her three sisters, and with two other mouths to feed she certainly must have struggled to survive and feed everyone. Nothing was more important to her than her children.

I don't know how Don felt about this period of his life, but he always spoke with great admiration and unabashed love for his mother and respect for his uncle and aunt who he lived with for several years. Often, Don recalled, he would be given a quarter, take his sister's hand, and off they'd go. He'd see to it that she was safe, and sometimes they would see a movie together before he made her dinner and put her to bed.

There were moments of childhood bliss and simplicity: playing soldier, cowboys and Indians, after-school days with hot cocoa and buttered toast spread out on a winter's day, reading encyclopedias for fun, or singing and dancing. He loved listening to the radio. We all experience only what is there before us, and we're shaped by those environmental experiences; it is all we know. One of these experiences would shape Don more than any other. He recounted this story to me many times, and could never get through it without tears:

> "Christmas 1949. Mom had finally gotten custody of Sandy and I. We were living in a one-room apartment above the 18th East Bar on 1st Avenue and 1st Street in Duluth. Mom was working at the Zelda Bar and Grill making chump change and meager tips. She worked nights so I was in charge of getting Sandy and I fed and in bed. When we woke up on Christmas morning we saw the top of a scrawny Christmas tree standing on a small table under the only window. Mom had strung popcorn on thread as decorations and two small packages were under the tree. Mom stood there in her tattered robe all of thirty years old with her hands clasped under her breasts, and a look of such hopeless hope that we would like our gifts . . . I'll never forget that."

Don told me he remembered watching her as she looked at the small pittance she could offer her children at that time. He remembered seeing her face—beautiful, sad, and worn—and in that moment Don knew that he would never ever give her a moment's heartache. He made a quiet promise to her in that very instant. She looked so young yet so defeated and that image of his sweet mother left an indelible imprint on his heart and inspired in him the need to always seek kindness. It was a pivotal moment between parent and child, and it shaped the strength of his character.

Each time that Christmas story came up for Don, whether in a conversation with someone else or just with me, I was reminded of a pivotal moment in my life with my father, which changed the trajectory of my dreams and desires. Both Don and I were impassioned by a desire to make our parents proud, and that shared heart made us the perfect complement for each other.

When I was younger I would chat with Dad in the bathroom while he was shaving. I loved to watch him shave. So one morning while Daddy was shaving and we were talking about this and that, he simply said, "I need you to go all the way, Nita." I replied, "Okay, Dad," in that moment making him a promise.

A college education was something my father wanted for all his children, but life can take us down different roads. I knew that as much as I wanted to do this for him, I also had to do it for myself. I wanted to make him proud—we all did, and have, since then—but that promise to my father built a new desire in me to excel.

I was a freshman college student and our sweet mother had died. My eldest sister had not finished college and was now married. My middle sister had done two years of college and her grieving was so great that she did not return for a while, but I wanted to fulfill the promise I made to my dad.

When my name was called to receive my bachelor of science in nursing, I wept with joy for both of us. I wanted to hand it to him and my sisters, who were as capable as I was. He had not had the opportunity to finish high school, and as I walked across that stage, I felt he walked right beside me. Fulfilling my promise to my dad to "go all the way" was a grand moment for us that I will never forget.

Later I became an ICU nurse because I thought they were the smartest. I was inspired to continue entering pageants even though for six years I only won runner-up, because I had to go "all the way" in every area of my life. But those words my Dad had spoken built a fire in me to be a winner, not a runner-up. Donnie and I shared that drive and desire to be the very best that we could be and we supported that passion in the other.

Not unlike what my father expected of me, Rubie always knew that Don was destined for greatness. She told me once that she had looked at his hands as a young boy and prophetically spoke that her son would never do manual labor. As a man, Don learned the voice-over business, gained a reputation, and eventually became known as one of the world's great voices, fulfilling his mother's prophecy. No parent was prouder of a child than Rubie was of Don, and she enjoyed her bragging rights.

He learned sound engineering in his army days and had the great opportunity to work with and record the United States Army Corp Band. His favorite memory of that time was getting to work with Steve and Eydie Gormé before he was twenty years old. After his four years in the army, he moved to New York and was "poorer than a church mouse." He told me he found temporary housing, ended up getting food poisoning, and was alone with bouts of puking and diarrhea for three days, sicker than sick. When he recovered he pulled himself up once again to move forward and get a job at National Recording Studios as a sound engineer/editor.

Late in 1962, Don was assigned to a young radio producer named Floyd L. Peterson, who was creating radio commercials for *Dr. Strangelove.* They worked so well together that, in January of 1963, Don joined Floyd Peterson, making it a two-man operation out of Floyd's apartment.

Over the next couple of years, the company grew to employ thirty people and it expanded into its own building, a carriage house on West 57th Street. Floyd L. Peterson, Inc. was one of the first companies to work exclusively in motion picture advertising. Prior to that time, most film promotion was done in-house by the studios. It was during this period that the format for the modern movie trailer was developed, and Don and Floyd were among the first to create the catch phrases that still dominate trailers: "In a world," "A one-man army," "Nowhere to run, nowhere to hide, and no way out" being some of them.

Floyd truly gave Don his start, yet it was a beginning for them both. I learned from Don that they were called "trailers" because they used to follow—or trail—movies. In other words, they followed the film, instead of beginning them as they do today. Don, who was a young hotshot, quick on his feet, and always good with words, was hired as a writer and editor which was on-the-job training for him. He quickly assimilated and began to hire some voice talent for spots he wrote.

In the early part of his career, he had the great privilege to hire the legendary Orson Wells three times. Don created the phrase "In a world" and though he never thought of announcing himself, he did step into the announcer booth when an employee didn't show up. Perhaps the encyclopedia memorizations, marathon movie watching, and sound engineering were all put to good use with this position. Who could have dreamed that many years after this first voice-over he would announce the very movie spots he wrote the copy for and edit years later? Life has a funny way of preparing us for what is to come.

Chapter 9

WHEN YOU BELIEVE

"There can be miracles when you believe though hope is frail, it's hard to kill.
Who knows what miracles you can achieve when you believe? Somehow you will."

—Whitney Houston/Mariah Carey

There have been times in my life when I believed in the possibility of something happening against tremendous odds. The fortitude established in my younger years kept my belief and resolve in the hope that Donnie would get well even though it seemed impossible. Looking back and thinking about how losing Donnie also cost me my voice for a time, I remember how the same challenging parts of my life gave me the opportunity to find it. I am so grateful for every experience I had that prepared me to use my voice during those days when Donnie lost his. Participating in pageants was one of those obstacles that pushed me to use my voice.

When I first signed up for pageants I remember looking around and feeling mildly surprised that I was the only black girl in the competition.

Surely I was not the only girl of color in the state or region with talent, a dream, and a need for scholarship money. It seemed that each of the six years I competed for, drove to, and hoped for the coveted title of Miss Louisiana, I was almost always the only black girl on the stage and my family the only brown faces in a sea of cream. I eventually came to expect the feeling—of being the "only" one.

Though I developed a reputation for being the one to beat in talent competitions, the other girls always had me in the swimsuit competition. I was so skinny my thighs didn't touch (like they do now!). Back then, the judges wanted to see legs with the three diamonds: tops of the inner tights, knees and calves touching (this preference has been removed from competitions). Try as I might, using my best turnout and squeezing my buttocks tight, I couldn't get anything to touch.

Regardless I never won the swimsuit competition. Lucky for me, the talent competition was fifty percent of the overall points yet I didn't win in the first twelve or so pageants I entered.

I interviewed well because my nursing curriculum taught me a technique called interpersonal relationship training so we could learn how to deal with and talk to patients. I watched the news and read *Newsweek* and *Time* to stay abreast of current events and political rhetoric. It was important to be literate and have an opinion on things going on in the world and locally. I didn't know my nursing training would serve me the way it did in the interview process, but my determination came from wanting to be learned and intelligent; that's infinitely more exciting than just another pretty face.

I believe now that I kept going back again and again to different pageants even when I didn't win because the quiet expectation existed that my winning was impossible. So maybe I was determined to conquer this unattainable goal, to break a glass ceiling that had never been cracked. Maybe it was the vague memory that when I was fifteen my mother tried to enter me into some local pageant in my hometown. For reasons that were unknown to me at the time, I was denied entry, which infuriated my mother. I was told later she felt it was because I was black, but she never told me that. The Miss America pageants and most pageants in the late '70s to early '80s were still rather lily-white. I was a curious and determined girl, and perhaps deep inside I wanted to "get in" to show them what my mother knew to be right and true; I was worthy of standing there with the rest of them and that "All-American" didn't only refer to white girls. That black is beautiful, smart, and talented too.

I loved the interview portion because I enjoyed talking to people and asking and answering questions; I never tired of it and rarely got tripped up. It was always interesting to me the questions people asked, why they asked, and the messages their body language sent. There were certain questions that were asked at all interview competitions, like "Why should we choose you to be Miss So-and-so?" Deep down I wanted to say, "Because I'm the freaking best contestant, you chauvinist pig!" But of course I could never say such an egotistical, sassy thing. Humility, core moral values, talent, and intelligence were part of the formula for the winner. So though I was genuine, I had to be my extra best. It was always known—in the South or perhaps in general—that to be black competing in a white world, you had to be twice as good as the other girls. It was the way it was.

In spite of all that, my ultimate favorite part of the whole process was always the talent segments. Of course, there was always a girl twirling a baton—sometimes a flaming one—tap dancing or en pointe, playing the piano with some lovely gown draped over the piano bench, or ventriloquism. But I couldn't wait for my chance to sing.

No audience in the world is as enraptured and appreciative as a pageant audience. If you had a high, long, or loud note, it got thunderous applause. If you did a couple pirouettes or a leap, played a gliss on the piano or harp, tap-danced or cart-wheeled the ending, it elicited wild applause. It was deceiving, because it made you think you were better than you really were. The support was unbelievable.

I was never made to feel like an outsider (excepting an incident at a Miss Watermelon pageant where I was called the n-word). And even though I was often the only black girl, and despite my not winning for many years the pageant coordinators and contestants welcomed me with warmth and respect always. I gave them the same in return. There were no threatening or mean-spirited girls within the pageant, and though some were my direct competition, it was never personal; though outside of this gowned cocoon, it was still the South.

The worst part for me during the season of pageants was seeing the other girls with their moms helping them bring their bagged gowns and flowered makeup bags into the assigned dressing rooms. They'd get a kiss and be on their way. I carried my own bag and loaded myself in. Mother had died. And though I knew my dad, sisters, and various aunts, uncles and cousins would be in the audience screaming and cheering me on, seeing other girls with their mothers was when I missed mine the most. I would stand backstage and listen for my Dad's habitual clearing of his throat (since grade school, this how he signaled his presence), and then I knew I could make it, that all was good because moving past the sadness of not having my mother, my family was there.

After two years of competing and not winning the local pageants, some people began to say to me, "I don't know why you keep trying. You know those white folks ain't gon' let you win!"

I would just smile and keep going, but it built a fire in me because I've never liked someone telling me what I could not do. My family always taught me what I could do, and it made me want it all the more. Every academic grade and every accolade was hard-earned and appreciated throughout my life.

After I won some local pagents and went to Miss Louisiana three times, I was finally ready to quit. I thought I'd hit a wall. My dad asked me to try one more time. He had a "good feeling" he told me. Having been the first runner up in '83, had I gone on to compete for Miss America I would have competed against Vanessa Williams (a great lady) and Suzette Charles (a dear friend). It seemed there was finally permission to let a black girl win after Vanessa did.

Actually, I say I was the first Miss Louisiana who happened to be black. What they didn't really get was that it wasn't a new title for me; I had been the first and only black girl for so many of these pageants it started to feel normal. When the crown was finally on my head, I realized I had been the first black girl in that arena long before they placed the crown on my coiffed head. And I thought of how proud my mother would be if she were standing there alongside my dad, for not giving up.

Losing my mother and enduring in the face of that loss became a critical lesson for me as I was forced to deal with losing my greatest love. Those difficult moments at pageants and during other events where I wished I had my mom taught me to depend on myself no matter what. This learning enabled me to more fully love Don and allowed for our relationship to blossom into the harmony that it was because I did not need to have a man in my life the way some women did. I chose Donnie, and he chose me: Our love was organic and real and based on mutual trust and support, not dependency and fear. The nature of our bond enabled me to speak for him when he couldn't speak for himself. And that was why I lost my voice when I lost him; I lost a part of myself. I lost my other half.

Chapter 10

A DREAM WITH YOUR NAME ON IT

"Stand tall don't you be afraid. You're sure to find your way. And when that voice that's deep inside you says to take a chance, that's what you've got to do . . . 'cuz there's a dream out there with your name on it."

—Jennifer Holliday

There were only single-seat chairs in the fifth floor waiting room. It was brightly lit with an elevator pinging frequently. There was simply no place to sleep. So I thought it wiser to at least try to get a few hours of sleep each night at home so that I could be fresh for whatever the next day would bring. On Donnie's fifth day at the hospital, my phone continued to be flooded with calls from those who wanted to know how he was doing. I was too exhausted to return them individually, so I sat down to write to all my prayer warriors.

Sent: Wed, 27 Aug 2008 11:52 pm

Subject: Re: Good News about Don

Don is still considered critical though he is stable right now. He is still on the respirator and deeply sedated. He is off all meds that were being used to raise his blood pressure but he is still on dialysis until his kidney function returns (caused by the meds to keep his pressure up). They changed the heparin to a similar drug because he developed an antibody to it. He turned his head in my direction this morning but soon after he fell back into this induced sedation. We have been blessed with amazing nursing and caring physicians who watch over him. Those are his improvement and they work to balance the circulation with the respirations his body requires. Still balancing that, but moving in the right direction. I sing to him every day even though he is not able to respond; he knows I'm there. Thank you for continued prayers and God walks with us through this. Your prayers mean so much and have penetrated the very walls of Don's hospital room and filled it with angels of light and hope and peace. From the deepest place in my heart, I thank you all for rescuing my family right now with your love and prayers. Pray on,

Nita and family

Each day I saw small but significant improvements in Don's condition. We were all encouraged at the sheer strength Don showed in the fight for his life, his fight to be here with us. Every small incremental improvement was cause to cheer and praise God.

The doctors reminded us gently that even though he seemed to be making progress, he might not survive. In my mind, this was their way of covering their behinds. That day, his long-time cardiologist and friend commented on how strong Don was having survived cardiogenic shock, which occurs when the heart is unable to supply enough blood to the organs of the body. This is as close as one can get to death; had Don not been in the hospital, I shudder to think how quickly he could have left us. Wow. No one had ever given us these words before and the fact that he was still with us what was nothing short of miraculous.

Still, at this point saying he might not survive was unreal—in my mind he was surviving. But they always have to tell you your loved one could die. When you call a doctor's office, they always advise you to call 911 if you have a "life-threatening emergency." But when you are in the fight for your life and health, or going through it, everything positive is promising. So we dismissed their remarks about our boy possibly leaving us. They didn't know him like I did. I even invited the doctors to look at a couple more YouTube videos because I wanted them to see Don in his funny, up-out-of-a-sick-bed, witty, super intelligent, irreverent, loving man even if only for three minutes.

Our friend Johnnie, who had given us the affirmation Don and I spoke to each other back in January, came to the hospital for a visit. Johnnie has a pure spirit and a deep connection with the Divine. After my WMDs (Women of Mass Destruction) mistook her for a stranger, we all shared a good laugh about my sisters not recognizing her. While she and I walked back to Don's room I prepared her to see Don in his still state.

I trusted her, and she went in and stayed alone in Don's room for about fifteen minutes. She came out filled with the Holy Spirit, speaking in tongues and walking along the corridor outside the ICU in a trance. When she was able to speak to us, she simply said to me with a smile, "His room is filled with angels."

I believed they were there to protect him. I couldn't have known, nor was I ready to accept, that they were there to carry him to the other side. Her words comforted me, as did her presence and certainty about the angels in Don's room. I knew she knew. Though the situation overall was overwhelming, this moment uplifted me and gave me hope. The pull and tug of the fragility of his life was a see-saw ride that day; the most noble and quietly fearful moments were tangled at that intersection. Life is filled with these bittersweet moments, those that hold both promise and fear in the same instance.

Any time we are at a crossroads—be it between life and death, or choosing one path over another—emotions will combine from opposite ends of the spectrum. Deciding to leave Shreveport to pursue my singing dream was one of these moments, both bitter and sweet. But I have learned to always be amazed by and open to what waits for us down the road that we chose. For me, it was my boy. My decision to leave was made with much thought, prayer, and talks with my Daddy, but the moment I was faced with leaving, was still very difficult.

A producer of a TV show called *Miss Hollywood* suggested to me after I won Miss Louisiana that I really should try to "go for it," referring to my singing career. He reminded me I could go back to nursing any time, but would always regret it if I didn't give singing a try. His words pushed me out of the comfortable bed of my life in Shreveport to get in my car and drive to Los Angeles, hoping for an open door as well as a voice of my own in that huge place.

Leaving what is familiar is like walking in mud: every step forward is a bit of a struggle. The predawn morning was warm and muggy as I headed toward my packed beige 190E Mercedes parked in the carport. I turned to hug my Daddy, who packed the car with me, to find him reaching toward me to return my hug. He gently bit my jaw, a sign of affection from him throughout my life.

My dad stood in the carport just beyond the kitchen's screen door and repeated what he'd always said to me since I went off to college.

"Now remember, if you go to a party and leave your drink, getcha self a new one. Don't drink that same one unless you took it witcha."

I nodded and he continued, "And know that there are many wolves in sheep clothing, so keep you eye and ears keen."

"Yes sir, Daddy," I said, trying to calm his fears for me.

"And don't put yourself in harm's way. Let somebody know where you are and don't go out late by yourself. And if it doesn't work out, you can always come home," he said.

I smiled and knew as I always did how much I was loved. Nothing in the world was more important to me than making my dad proud. He was proud of all his children and he and my mother raised us to be kind, thoughtful citizens. I also knew that something beyond my Cedar Grove community was calling to me. Little did I know it was the discovery of both my new voice and my greatest love. I carry that promise to "go all the way" in my heart to this very day. That promise added volumes to my will to achieve my dreams.

It was time. As I pulled out of the carport where my Daddy stood waving at the end of the driveway, my heart was both sad and excited. The freshly cut grass on damp summer mornings, the smell of hair being pressed across the street at Ms. Cookie's house where women's laughter and stories seeped through the door and window of her home beauty shop, dogs barking behind chain-link fences, the night symphonies of crickets and cicadas, the friendly faces in every house on my block— all I had known was suddenly in my rear-view mirror. Ahead of me was unknown, unexplored territory. Like a pioneer girl, I headed for a place I barely knew. It was scary and exhilarating at the same time. I didn't know how I was to accomplish my big dreams, but I would try my best. But even then I knew my angels were with me.

I now know, of course, that one of the biggest reasons I was headed to LA was to meet my soul mate and love of my life.

I arrived in Los Angeles on August 26 that year, which I couldn't have known was Don's birthday. I had $250 to my name, a job working twelve-hour shifts as an ICU nurse at Brotman Medical Center, an apartment shared with three other nurses, and a big dream to sing. I didn't know my prince—on his way to his own big dreams— would show up in the form of a five-foot eight-inch white man who looked nothing like the prince I had imagined as a little girl (someone who looked like my dad or more handsome if possible), yet Don was my prince indeed. He was handsome yes, but not brown, and he had no horse except a cool candy-apple red and gray Jaguar. But he had the bluest eyes I had ever seen, the blue of a cloudless, breezy, early summer day. Both of us were on an unknown journey, and our voices would ultimately connect us.

Once I arrived in Los Angeles, a new friend, Tony Warren, took me to meet a man named Ed at a club called the Rose Tattoo. It was off of Santa Monica Boulevard in West Hollywood, on Robertson Street. Tony had been the winner of an ongoing singing competition. He brought me there and got me on the show. Armed with my pageant gowns, my new friend, and my voice, I was excited to sing for my first Los Angeles audience.

Five steps below street-level, right off the parking lot on Robertson, a gay bar during the week was transformed on Sunday nights into a place where young singers could work and compete for their dream to be heard in the business. It was a small, dimly lit cabaret-style room with mirrored walls, small round tables covered with white cloths, dark red leather booth seating, and one long table in the center for the judges. There was a small stage with pre-fixed gel lighting and room enough for a tight trio (piano, bass and drum) and a singer's microphone on a stand. There was also an elevated sound booth against the wall to the left of the stage—used to DJ while in bar mode—and surrounded by a wooden door.

The competition was called "Stardom Pursuit." I knew a lot about competition from my pageant years, and my several attempts to get onto *Star Search,* so none of it frightened me. I'd had my share of "yes, but not now." I was ready.

I was a lanky twenty-six-year-old five foot ten inch, one hundred twenty-five-pound girl, with a scepter, crown, and a closet of beaded and sequined gowns. For my first night, I chose a green sequined halter-back gown with a taffeta fish tail. I picked up Tony from his Hollywood apartment and we drove to the Rose Tattoo. Inconspicuous we were not as we walked toward the back of the bar. In heels I was nearly six two and Tony was six four.

It was a magical feeling for me as I walked down those steps into the club that night. After finally winning Miss Louisiana, I'd been devastated when I didn't receive any notice or awards from Miss America, or the national exposure I had hoped for. But right now I was focused on the fact that within two weeks of my arrival, I'd been lucky enough to have the opportunity to try opening a new door in Los Angeles.

I stood when my name was called, headed to the stage for my turn, and listened to my introduction.

"All the way from Louisiana, and a former Miss Louisiana, making her West Coast debut, please welcome . . . "

I remember thinking of my sweet Daddy and family who supported me as I pursued my dream from plays to pageant. Countless miles, audiences, gowns, and pumps later, I carried their spirit onto the stage with me and stood looking into the crowd of new faces, simply hoping they would like my voice. Once again I had to prove myself, as I would have to over and over again in my career. That I could sing was a given; my voice had become one of the ways I defined myself. But with the *Star Search* rejections and my disillusionment with pageants, my self-esteem was a little bruised. I could hear my Mamma saying, "Just sing from your heart, Nita." And in that lime green sequined dress, I sang my two songs: Aretha Franklin's "Respect" and Sheena Easton's "When He Shines."

I'd learned that most people, seeing my slender frame, expected to hear a slender, sweet voice. So when I belted out "Whatchu want!" with the voice of a big girl, the audience's collective gasp followed by smiles and rhythmic nodding to the beat were familiar to me.

Next came the ballad, and the faces began to look even more familiar as they softened with the song. There was some hand-waving and nods of approval and delight that inspired me to go higher. But there was one very special set of blue eyes twinkling up at me. Suddenly I felt I was in a room full of new friends. Both songs received standing ovations, which nearly brought me to tears and built my self-esteem.

Tony escorted me off-stage when I finished, stopping to introduce me to a short, blue-eyed man, but not before whispering to me that this man was very generous and would give you the shirt off his back—literally.

Don rose, extended his hand, and we exchanged a smile and firm, warm handshake. Then I listened to his melodious, melted-butter-falling-out-of-his-face voice saying how much he had enjoyed my singing. I was polite, but thrilled at this compliment and received it with a heartfelt thank you. Of course I did not know I would spend the next twenty-two years with a man who would tell me how wonderful I was, and my gratitude for being loved that way expanded me to become what I hoped he saw me to be. Love does that: you rise to meet each other—not to control, just to elevate.

Making my way to my car that early September night, I felt good. I didn't know where it would lead, but at least I was singing. I stopped working Sundays so I could go back and sing for the rest of the competition. I still didn't know how I would find singing work that paid, or an agent to help me. I also didn't know I had just met the man who would become the love of my life. Perhaps he knew it, but I didn't have a clue. I have a sense my angels did . . .

I was so broke that my nurse's paycheck still left me short. Soon after moving into the Oakwood apartments, I got a Los Angeles welcome by way of a broken car window and stolen radio while it was parked in the garage. Times were very lean for this newcomer. The land of milk and honey sure didn't feel that way as I started needing to shell out money I didn't have.

My former employer had been a Catholic hospital run by a group of nuns. Out of the blue these angels sent me a check for $500 to support my dreams. It was an Angel Intervention!

The stakes were high going into the singing competition. I needed the $2500 I would get if I won to get financially caught up, and I hoped winning would increase my visibility in the business and offer me further opportunities.

Don's small video company was taping the event, preparing for the finals held in a ballroom at what is now the London Hotel in West Hollywood. I noticed Don would always sit near me and make me laugh with his witty off the wall comments and jokes. He'd say in a note, "Nita, I dream of kissing you but I think of the ladder and the oxygen to get there," then he'd quietly giggle with eyebrows raised and mischief bouncing from his blues. I thought he was a funny guy and didn't seem as much of the playboy I had thought at my first glance with his open shirt, medallion, and fancy car. There was sweetness in his smile.

I won that competition in mid-October that year and the tears I cried were of joy at being able to pay my bills! From that I was given representation, so I began going for auditions early the next year.

After the Sunday night sing-offs at the Rose Tattoo (performances there were ongoing), Don would invite a group of us back to his bachelor pad where he had a karaoke "singing machine," and we'd continue the singing in the lower level of his living room with its round open fireplace, way past midnight. He'd even sing— usually a Neil Diamond song. It was a fabulous house and a fun hangout. He was always a gentleman, but seeing his amazing home with black lacquered floors and a red door, I was more certain than before that he either had a revolving door, or was gay. Either way, I wasn't interested and I certainly didn't think he was looking at me. He seemed to be the kind of guy that would have a leggy blond on his arm to ride in his swanky car with, not this green, been-burned-before black girl with big dreams. Much later, he would become the main player in the evolution of that dream.

One of those Sunday evenings, he sat close to me and said, "I like the concept of you."

What a strange and different come-on line, I thought, *but at least he's intelligent.* Not the standard, "Can I have yo' number?" That kind of lame come-on was a complete turn-off to me. And Don was so kind, offering his home to all of us. I began to see over time a different man than what he presented. We became friends, though I never went to his house alone. I always dragged my buddy Tony with me since he sang, too. Then I booked my first professional job with Ben Vereen as a background vocalist and off I went. It was a very exciting time for me professionally.

Don's and my friendship grew deeper, and I found myself caring about how he was doing during the day. Though he had a small editing company, he was booking three to five voice-over sessions a day. He showed himself to be a man of high integrity and kindness. I began to see his generosity around me and with others. He tried to give me gifts that I would give back. It took awhile for me to learn that the fun for him wasn't in how much money he made, but how much fun he had enjoying it and sharing his good fortune. He was generous with all who knew him. I didn't want him to think I could be bought, nor did I want to feel like I owed anyone anything. He once told me he got the most joy out of the giving. I thought he was being really smooth but I would learn he was speaking his truth, and generosity was a big part of him.

Our friendship caught fire and soon we only wanted to see each other. Don asked me out to dinner in December, and our first date was in January 1987. The more I got to know him, the more I really began to like him. He was a man, not a boy, trying to find himself. There were fleeting, can-this-work moments on our early dates, but I felt so comfortable with him I could be myself completely.

I remember getting butterflies in my stomach hearing his voice on the phone. I thought, *"Really, Nita . . . are you falling for this guy?!"*

I think the word is "giddy." I looked forward to knowing that I would hear from him. His voice melted me like butter in a hot skillet. But I didn't want to let him know I was beginning to have these feelings just yet; I wanted to watch and figure out if he felt the same way too. I didn't think I could fall in love by myself.

He told me one day that he'd called up all the girlfriends and told them that he'd met "the one." I had no idea he had done that. I was smitten and scared a bit, because I had not expected to fall for him, but I did. I fell in love with his heart. He was a hopeless romantic and had candlelight, roses, and music whenever I visited. He wrote beautiful poems for me, but his kindness grabbed my heart. He adored surprising me because I have big reactions to things. The playboy image began to melt away and the loving man rose to meet me; we wanted to spend all our time together.

Don was married when I met him, but he explained that it was in name only. That did not settle well with me, and I told him early on that if he wanted to be with me, he needed to be free. He was concerned about his responsibilities to his family. Though he'd been living in a different city from his wife for nearly six years when we met, he told me he was working on it. I thought, *How much more working on it is there?* And he had his daughter who had a difficult time being a pawn in their broken relationship.

But we were a new, beautiful thing that surprised and caught both of us off guard. I think he liked to use the fence of his being married as protection. There was so much guilt associated with his marriage, yet he always tried to do the right thing by his family.

In October of '87, Don still hadn't filed for divorce, and though we were crazy for each other, I left him. Morally, I could not continue in a relationship with him. He filed two days later. I believed it was past time he did it. I didn't want to get married; I just wanted him not to be.

We knew we wanted to be together, but Don had some hurdles. He stopped snorting cocaine and doing other self-destructive behaviors and finally, fully stepped into his life without the false protection of an empty marriage that he felt stuck in.

I was surprised that all I had to do was ask him to stop doing something harmful to himself, and he did—as if he just needed someone to tell him no. He called me his angel and told me many times that I'd saved his life. While I cherished the notion, I believe Don was such a good soul God would have sent an angel to him anyway; I'm just glad He picked me.

Chapter 11

OUR LOVE

"Our love will stand tall as the trees, our love will spread as wide as the sea, our love will shine bright in the night like the stars above and we'll always be together."

———Natalie Cole

When Don and I first fell in love, we were consumed with each other; there was never enough time together and never enough words to share. The exact moment that I knew our love was bigger than both of us wasn't a fireworks moment but a knowing that we couldn't wait to see each other, the quiet comfort of getting to see him at the end of a day when I was in town, or the sound of his rich baritone on the phone heightening the anticipation of being in his company and laughing.

Don was a man's man, with a chivalrous, kind, old Hollywood school of charm and class. He loved to dress well and open the door for me; he believed in romance and loved the element of surprise. His adventurous spirit was contagious and he could get me to be excited about anything he was excited about.

It was April of 1987 when I told Don I didn't want to see anyone else. I thought I was going out on a thin limb to say this, but he made it clear to me he hadn't seen anyone else since our first date! I found that difficult to believe because he was so charming and witty he could be with any kind of woman. Someone shorter and white . . . maybe even a blond. (Didn't gentlemen prefer blonds?) With my pressed-and-curled black hair, I was intelligent but not savvy—I was just me.

There were times early on in our courtship when we were aware of people staring at us, trying to figure us out. If we were dressed for an event, guys would smirk as though they were thinking, "This white guy has a willowy call girl." Black guys would look lustfully at me as though I was another sistah taken by the white man. All of which I found insulting but never intimidating because as our love grew Donnie and I didn't notice those eyes as much; we were clear and calm about who we were no matter what we looked like to anyone else.

I remember a particular incident when we were leaving the Wang Theater in Boston in early1988. I had just performed in a show with Ben Vereen, my then employer. I wore my tight black costume dress and heels, and Don, in a tux, held my hand on the way back to our hotel. We were engaged by then, and a group of white men in suits standing on the sidewalk looked over and nodded that "oh yeah, you got you call girl" look.

I flashed my two-carat engagement ring (Yes, two carats.) as we sauntered by and simply said, "Engaged!"

Boy that felt good.

Don told me that once when he called his mother to tell her he had found "the one," her first reaction was, "Does she have to be black?" because she had already heard of me. That was said in all innocence because she really didn't know that many black people since she'd lived in Duluth for most of her life. I think we (black people) find it too frigging cold in Duluth to stay there.

His reply was simply, "Wait until you meet her."

On my side of the family, I wondered if my Dad—being a product of the racially divided Jim Crow South and Jim Crow laws as a young man—would accept this older white man that I had started dating. Don had impressed my sisters with a full turkey dinner complete with his famous mashed potatoes when they came to visit me. He charmed them, and I'm sure they gave my Dad a good report. I was so pleased and inspired by my Dad after I called to tell him that I was dating a "white guy." I tried to sneak it in during a fast-paced conversation, thinking he might have some objection or tell me I needed to be careful.

His reply was, "He treats you nicely? Then that's all that matters, then."

Neither of us initially wanted to get married, but love grabbed our hearts and our souls danced as though we'd known each other for a lifetime, and we knew we had to become man and wife.

After proposing in April 1988, Don said, "Are you kidding me? I'm not letting you go!" And he never did. We were married October 1, 1988, in the garden of the Four Seasons Hotel in Beverly Hills. I had worked ten straight twelve-hour shifts in two weeks to help with the cost of the wedding and to pay for bridesmaid's dresses. I didn't want Don paying for everything just because he made more money than I did. It was important that I contribute what I could.

Our wedding was a grand affair with a four-camera shoot. Our wedding party was nearly twenty people strong, and every couple down the aisle was interracial like we were. Don was involved in every step of the process, down to the seating arrangements. Ben Vereen and Steve Susskind were our best men and I heard people asking as I walked into the room, "Is this a real wedding or a television show?" when they saw Ben and the cameras.

I remember clearly that sunlit mid-morning sky as I walked into the garden on the arm of my handsome father, rounding the corner to walk down the aisle after the flower girls had laid petals on the walkway. All heads turned toward me and they quietly rose to their feet from the white folding chairs on the grass. It was as though the angels had choreographed it. I can still hear the birds chirping in that moving, quiet, reverent moment.

There was so much love streaming in my direction that I overflowed in tears. My daddy kept saying, "Smile baby!" through his smiling teeth, but by the time we got to the place where he was to give me away with Pastor Larry standing there, I had to swipe at the tears dripping from my chin with the back of my hand. Yes, a classy moment indeed.

We wore body microphones in true LaFontaine style. Reverend Dr. Larry Keene married us, and his beautiful, meaningful ceremony helped us tightly and lovingly tie our love-knot. His words of wisdom, insight, and blessing stayed with us all the days of our marriage. We lit the unity candle to the beautiful words of "Two Different Worlds" from *West Side Story:* "Now our two different worlds are one." ("We's married now!")

More than four hundred guests witnessed our love and perfect harmony that blessed day. The reception and sit-down dinner was a show worth paying for. Our talented friends sang, and a live band performed. To top it all, Ben gave us a half-hour show in which I ran on stage in my gown with my background singer friends and sang the parts to "Stand by Me" while Ben danced on a table. It was an amazing day and I thought I couldn't love Don more, but I was wrong.

Being married to Don was like being at an amusement park. There were thrill rides and carousels, and music in the air along with the excitement of waiting in line for the next wild ride. There were also gentler rides in life with him that were lovely too: the small, sacred, only-witnessed-by-us moments. I was happy to join his adventurous spirit and ride with him. I think I brought in a little conservatism, but often we met in the middle. We both loved fun and adored laughing.

A few months before our wedding, Don called me at work to let me know that he'd found a house for us. Well, that was great, except I wanted to be part of the decision! Don was not one to wait for things. He came, he saw, he conquered! But I saw and loved it; it was a new beginning for us both. It needed some work, but we would do that together, too, when we got back from our honeymoon.

We were taken by limo to the airport after our blissful wedding day and enjoyed a romantic, loved-filled honeymoon on Rangiroa, Tahiti, a tiny island in the South Pacific. The resort was charming and we brought Scrabble, our favorite game and pastime. The night sky was fireworks-worthy: there were so many stars I had never seen before, and very little pollution. It was a spectacular, serene piece of heaven with crystal clear waters, great food, and time to get used to being called Mrs. LaFontaine.

We moved into our new home upon our return and with the help of our trusted housekeeper Connie—who'd been with Don for eight years—and some close family members, we moved in and set up the kitchen and bedrooms. It was a four-bedroom home at the top of Crescent Heights with a city view, a pool, great master suite (huge closet), and an open floor plan. The walls needed old wallpaper removed and new paint. The carpeting needed changing and we wanted to get some new furniture. But it had all the things we love in a home: lots of natural light, a well-appointed kitchen with Spanish tiles, and good flow of space for the parties we enjoyed throwing.

Two weeks after moving in, I was off to Germany for a record development deal with a producer named Thilo. I was away for three weeks working on music and some performances (I sang on the same stage as Milli Vanilli . . . yep I said Milli Vanilli), but we promised each other we would never ever be apart that long again. We were miserable and longed for each other. Don's days were full; he was averaging at least seven to ten sessions a day now, but we spoke every night. We were so happy to be together when he picked me up from the airport and I was even happier to be home with my man. When we got closer to home, a mischievous twinkle appeared in his eyes and I knew he'd been up to something.

When I walked in the front door, it was a different house. Don had painted, recarpeted, and bought new furniture, giving our place a full facelift. I remember going back to the front door to check the address because it looked so different.

It was so Donnie. After the surprise, I was a bit peeved because I wanted to be a part of the process in our first home. Still learning the man, I had forgotten that he'd furnished his entire two-bedroom apartment in one day when he moved to LA from New York. "I'll take that, two of those, that one there and three of . . . Does that come in orange? Have it delivered today."

That was how he worked and that was how he shopped. He had given the fancy Corvette to my sister Kathy because it had always been her dream car and we purchased a van, thinking he could rest between sessions in the back of it.

He came up with the idea to get a limo because his work was growing rapidly now; parking and traffic were tremendous stressors as he tried to get from one place to another. Don said, "It will pay for itself."

I balked and fussed at such an outrageous, ostentatious idea, and talked with my dad. He said some words I'll never forget. "Nita, the man is trying to live. Live with him!" Our love grew exponentially in the time we were apart. It was lovelier now than the wedding day and each decision we made together brought us closer, even when we didn't agree.

One year, eight months, and two weeks after our wedding, Skye was born. In a chapel in Hana, Maui, we had prayed out loud on our first anniversary. Don had not been sure he wanted to become a dad again, feeling he'd not done such a great job with his firstborn. He was concerned about being an older father, too. I reassured him that he would become our child's standard and everyone else would be compared to him. That was prophetic in a way I didn't know. But in that little chapel, he asked out loud for God to give us a baby. Eight months and two weeks later he was rubbing my back with tennis balls and helping me with my Lamaze breathing. He was there every step of the way. He hadn't had this privilege when his Chrissy was born because fathers were not allowed in the delivery room then.

When we heard Skye's first cry, Don's face lit up. He'd chosen the name Skye (boy or girl) from the moment we knew a baby was on the way. We didn't know her gender until she was born. He held her and looked at her with such love and amazement. He bathed her and sang to her as he washed warm water over her new little squirmy body as overhead lights were lowered and soft music played.

We were both crying, his tears hanging on the tip of his nose. I felt he couldn't believe he was getting another chance and family, and I couldn't believe how much more I loved him at that moment for the way he looked at her. And again, four years later when little Liisi, born by C-section, was handed to us, my putty Daddy boy Don was a wet, sobbing mess at the sight of our second child, highlighting all the things she could do that no other baby could. A mother grows another heart each time she has a child, but her love for their father is expanded. Our lives become more united in the creation of a family.

There were morning and bedtime rituals, rules, and manners taught in our home. We created a fun home where the children were allowed to be children; a place where other kids didn't want to leave and our children felt safe to express every emotion. There was a playhouse in the backyard, riding razors or roller-skating in the house, jumping on the bed (with supervision), eating with their fingers, singing for their supper, even the freedom to run naked if they chose! We also taught them to use their words and speak up for themselves and their friends, but to try to be kind in all things.

Laughter was our family's theme music. A day in our house looked to most like a sitcom combining the Cosby's and *All in the Family,* from the silly to the sublime. One of our friends said we were just "too damn happy!" when asked why he didn't stay with us when he visited from out of town.

We were blessed, and we knew and honored that. But our life and love were real, true, lovely, and entertaining. With my breaking into song at any given moment and Don's incredible wit, jokes, and playful spirit (he was a master prankster and loved slapstick comedy), joy abounded. Though we had simple nights when we just ate dinner (with no TV), helped with homework and baths, there was always something to laugh about.

Don was never without a book. He had to own them, so he made frequent trips to the bookstore, often coming home with a Santa-sack full of them. They were his friends. In the back of the limo, at the bedside, in the bathroom—he had to have a book. His appetite for them was voracious.

When Skye was a toddler, she'd lay in her little bed at three with her index finger across her lips reciting her memorized books, just like Dad did. Skye enjoyed reading as much as her dad and eventually wanted to read by herself.

Liisi was his little "dolly." He adored having her little doe-eyed thumb-sucking, ear-holding presence right near his heart. He hardly ever put her down.

Don and I loved nightly bedtime stories with the girls, then they finally asked us not to read to them anymore. We sometimes sat in their darkened rooms and told stories without books, making it up as we went. Don created a series called Princess Skye and Liisi and the Farting Horse. I'd chime in with some magical creature voice to add to the drama and suspense. He could make the sound of a fart or a burp with his deep voice and the girls would squeal with delight and laughter.

Some days he would take the girls to work with him. That was always a treat for them because there were super sugary goodies at the studios that I would never have allowed. One morning before Liisi was born, Skye wanted to "play Daddy." After pulling on her pretend pants, she went down a little hall and sat, brought her index finger and thumb together like she had seen her Dad do a hundred times, covered her left ear with her hand, and announced, "Coming tonight on NBC!" Where were the cameras when I needed them?

A ritual Don started twenty years before with his first daughter, Chrissy, was to "blow a happy dream." He would gently blow into the girls' open mouths; and they would swallow his breaths, ensuring good dreams.

We were falling deeper in love, and we were madly in love with our family. I was always grateful for my children's health and the peace, love, and stability that was my home life. When the world or work seemed out of control or unreasonable, coming home to them was beautiful and fulfilling. Don and I had date nights (not often enough), discussions, and made decisions in our tub-for-two.

There was a magical quality to the lives of our children, and we helped to foster their wonder. We taught them to add a positive touch when people asked them "What are you?" In Sweden, children of mixed races are called golden nuggets. So many of the terms that permeated our country had come from the "one drop" rule in the Deep South and had so many negative connotations for children. We decided to give them a word that held beauty and light, like the love they were conceived in.

When her friends asked Skye what she was, she said she was a princess. At further insistence, she would explain that her mother was brown and her daddy was peach, so that made her golden. The kids got it and moved on to their play. Ahh, the beauty of childhood and the simplicity of explanations during innocence.

Whether building our dream home, making a feature movie with the girls, remodeling our home, choosing our pets, adding a home studio, or planning our next vacation "adventure," there was always something going on with the LaFontaines. Flying helicopters, hot air ballooning, and glider plane rides were a game for Don and I was happy to join the fun. He never lost his inner boy, yet never put much value in things except the fun in getting them. He enjoyed toys and gadgets and the pursuit of them, and he wanted his loved ones to enjoy them, too. He gave many of his first cell phones and fax machines as gifts because he wanted dear friends to enjoy the things that he had. If there was a new gadget, he wanted to be the first to have it. But he always bought one for Charles, his birthday brother and dear friend, and others, too.

His family was sacred and he loved the home we built together. That "He who has the most toys wins" was his life's subtext; it was the boy in him, and I was continually intrigued, fascinated, and falling deeper in love with.

One of the traits that continually fascinated me about Don was his ability to change. When we met, he had a closet lined with expensive Georgiou slacks worth a couple hundred dollars a pair. Though he had been raised with meager means, one of the ways he treated himself was with well-made clothing. I was brought up shopping the sale racks, and knew how to find bargains, so I re-introduced him to Marshall's, Ross, and sales racks even though he kept his nice slacks and jackets.

He would say, "Nita, you get what you pay for."

He preferred well made things, but I knew how to find the same items in discount stores.

His mind was so agile and filled with information that he referred to it as "useless information central."

We held each other's hand and marveled at our life together. I had the tall and dark and he had the handsome. We were a team, a loving pair like Bacall and Bogart, Luke and Laura, Hepburn and Tracy. He was one of those rare people whose character matched his gifts. His heart was as voluminous as his booming talent. He was my calm in the storm and I was his life raft of reason; we complemented each other perfectly.

We loved helping others, too. Our blessings were bountiful and we knew we were to be blessings to others. There was a young lady at our church who was blind but led a very independent life. Don found one of the first computers that could type what she spoke and surprised her with it. There were many other times we helped others, but he always preferred to be an anonymous giver. We adored and searched for ways we could be of service to others. This was part of our destiny together as a couple.

People held up our love as the example of what love should be: big, fun, and filled with light. We knew how blessed we were to have each other.

Chapter 12

BRING HIM HOME

"God on high, hear my prayer in my need you have always been there . . .
bring him home."

———————

—*Les Misérables*

Though our pasts, my life, and our family were constantly on my mind, I was firmly mired in the present, as I dealt with Don's doctors and medical procedures while he was in the hospital battling for his life. I wanted to make sure my boy got the best treatment, which I believe was their intention. I did not want our life together to end and I was doing everything in my power to keep him here with me—with us. Writing emails to my prayer village was helpful for me, as it forced me to reflect on the day's doings and occurrences. While I wrote I was enveloped in the light and sounds of people chanting and praying for us. During those writing moments when I reflected and spoke for Don, the lights and sounds of his sick room were drowned out.

August 30, 2008

Dear prayer warriors,

I hope that I honor your prayers and love by letting you know the latest happenings on Don. We've been seeing incremental improvements daily with him and today is more of that. He is off of the constant dialysis and has it only when he needs it determined by certain lab values; that means he is a lot more stable. He is still heavily sedated and intubated but tomorrow Paul Pape and I will be bring lots of pics in to cover the walls of his room and fill it with even more tactile love and light. When he wakes he can see familiar things and faces. He is taking a few breaths on his own and is making some urine (not huge amounts but some is a lot better than none). He is still in very serious condition but every day he amazes us all. He has been deeply sedated so he's nowhere near awake yet but sedation is being decreased; all baby steps toward improvement. I've had all of your prayers and love, my family and a friend surrounding me and the girls and that has helped more than I can say. We feel the prayers and we see the prayers all around us working! They continue to reverberate through the walls of his room and send healing light as those collective prayers go up. Please continue to shout them up because we know that healing happens in God's time. So we watch and wait with a grateful heart.

Onward to healing,

Nita and family

It had been seven days since Don was admitted and I was worried about the damage the endotracheal tube was doing to his vocal chords. I had not heard his voice since the evening of the twenty-second. For Don, his voice was like an organ—as necessary to him as his heart and, in fact, connected to it in a way unlike any other. I put a call into Dr. Nasseri who had taken care of Don's voice most recently. He suggested it might be time to put in a trach to connect the ventilator below the vocal chords instead of the tube constantly splitting them and perhaps causing some friction or ulceration on his chords. We didn't get around to doing this but the seed was planted that it was something we needed to do sooner rather than later. The doctors felt it was difficult to put him through any kind of procedure because he was so fragile. But even then, after seven days, I was still focused on and thinking about him living, not dying.

He was becoming more stable with each passing day. The vasopressor meds were taken off and he was making clear yellow urine again. He was "holding his own" as we like to say in medicine. We saw these as huge signs that he was moving toward better health, starting on this seventh day of his stay in the hospital. I am reminded upon reflection that in the Creation story, God rested on the seventh day. We, too, felt that we could exhale and rest a little bit even as we were jubilant about his progress.

His blood pressure and heart rate were steady and stable, blood oxygenation was at a respectable level and his overall medications were being reduced including the intravenous steroids. These were all positives and improvements from those first dark days. The ventilator was still constant in an effort to give his other organs and especially his lungs time to recover from the trauma they'd been through and he was still heavily sedated as he lay under another clean white sheet.

My sisters and my father had to get back to their lives and work. Since Don was improving they felt it was safe to leave. Aunt Lillian stayed because I was still spending a great deal of my time at the hospital. It was nice to know she was at home for my girls so I could tend to their Daddy.

My father went in and talked to Don before he left for the airport. He told him, "All right, Son, I'm gonna see you soon. You keep on fightin', ya hear? Pappa prayin' for ya'." He kissed Don on the forehead for what would be his last time. Their love and respect for each other was powerful and deep. My father thought of Don as a son, despite their different backgrounds and experiences. A parent's love is truly amazing. In addition to the incredible blanket of love from those around us, the strength and power of our faith was an incredible support beam holding us.

Our little Brown Church Don and I were a part of grew and merged into a bigger, newer place called Church of the Valley. As it grew, so did Don's and my commitment to it. Both our girls were dedicated in a ceremony there. The church was in a Camelot period, with some of the most stellar people worshipping at a church that was intelligent, inclusive, diverse, and loving. The music ministry was phenomenal, and the stewardship, leadership, and teaching of Pastor Keene helped us all to develop together as a church family.

During the tenth anniversary celebration for Pastor Larry, Don—being The Voice—was asked to speak about him. He did so in a speech he did not run by me. I never worried but frequently provided disclaimers because I never knew what my unpredictable, irreverent husband was gonna say! But he totally took my breath away when he asked Pastor Larry to re-baptize him at the end of his speech. I stood up with tears streaming down my face and love pouring from my being. He had made this choice for himself and for our family. It was and still remains one of my most cherished memories.

My father flew out for his baptism. Don's faith was reborn, reconfirmed (since his days as an altar boy in Catholic church), and restored in this diverse church on a residential street in the Valley. What a glorious time this was for us all. This faith community was an anchor and foundation through many tough moments in our lives. Don took to it with his whole heart, becoming involved on the board and contributing not just finances but time and energy. I am so grateful for our shared faith in those last days of Donnie's life. I will always be comforted by my boy's commitment to God.

We had to call on our faith in a renewed way during the harsh days of Don's illness and hospitalization. It was a buoy for my family, and I really wanted to speak my prayer right. I knew Don would not want to be here on earth if he could not be Don. I was asking a lot in my prayers when I asked for him to be restored to us whole. I knew we had a long road back to wholeness, but I was up for the task. "In sickness and in health" was one of my vows to him and I meant it when I first said it, and more so every day of our lives together. We'd had other health challenges during our marriage but they were only speed bumps. I was with him, always praying and asking for guidance, and grateful for my medical knowledge in those times. Here I was again with my most earnest and fervent prayer that this wonderful foot soldier of goodness be healed. I think I prayed more for our daughters than myself, but my heart longed to see him well, even though the situation wasn't presenting a pretty picture.

Chapter 13

END OF THE ROAD

"Come to the end of the road, still I can't let go.
It's unnatural, you belong to me, I belong to you."

———

—Boyz II Men

A friend gave me the gift of inviting me to a healing ceremony for Don. I accepted having decided I was open to all paths of healing for my boy. The idea was that being in a space to receive healing myself could perhaps open a new window in Don's healing. Although this form of healing was outside my church, I know that receiving God's blessings doesn't always come through the doors of a church; the possibilities are all around us if we can open ourselves to them.

For the seven days since Don had been in the hospital, I started my mornings going directly to the hospital. Family and friends then joined us for short and long visits in the waiting room as I tended to my husband; some wanted to visit with Don and others simply wanted to be close by.

On that sunny last day of August, I drove to my friend's home on a tree-lined street in the Valley, where I met two other beautiful people filled with light and love for me and my family. Not knowing what to expect, I did know it wasn't witchcraft or anything else weird; it would simply be a different experience.

The healers explained that together they would offer healing for my body so that I could take that force with me back to Don. Once the session started, they began to pray and chant for me while touching my heart and head. All the while, my inner monologue was praying for Don and for our children; that he would be healed and brought back to us fully. I expected a miracle, as we'd had many since we'd begun our slow dance with cancer. I wanted one more—a big one.

The chanting sounded like beautiful hymns I did not know, repetitive rhythmic words. Near the end of the session, they asked me to lie on the floor and again touched my head and my heart and added some new chants and prayers. I felt lighter, and—for the moment—peaceful.

There was a digital clock on the floor at the top of my head. When the session stopped, my friend commented, "Hmmm . . . I've never seen that happen before; the clock went to all zeros. That's a sign of a new life beginning."

I didn't know what to make of that statement, but I took it to heart. It reminded me of the day when a different, unrelated friend told me that she'd dreamed of Don getting out of the bed and putting on his clothes. She took it as a sign of him getting better and leaving the hospital; I took both comments as positive omens and perceptions.

They offered me a delicious home-cooked vegetarian meal to bridge our energy and focus after the healing ceremony. I had an urgent sense I should get to Don's bedside, but I didn't want to be rude so I stayed for a short while. But I couldn't restrain the feeling, and had to leave.

Upon my arrival, I went directly to be with Don and noticed immediately he'd developed a low-grade fever. He'd not had a fever before today, and the doctors covering his care expressed concern that his blood pressure was very low, and dropping. They had to put him back on the vasopressor, which slowed his urine flow once more.

I thought, *This is not what we want to happen on day eight, dammit.*

Don had several large-bore IV's going into his body, which can be a portal of entry for bacteria no matter how careful or skilled the nursing care. The doctor on duty that day was not the usual one, but he worked to try to balance Don's vital body processes, first by giving him large boluses (sometimes five hundred to one thousand ccs) of IV fluids in an effort to keep his blood pressure at a somewhat functional level; it kept dropping dangerously low.

For the entire twelve-hour shift, Don's vital signs were up and down. It became clear that the extra IV fluids were not working for him. In this part of the fight for his life, the wife in me still held on to a thread of hope even as he began to look weaker. A fever and low blood pressure are a deadly combination I knew from my years of nursing. The large-bore needles—which I felt were the source of his temperature spike—were still in place, and I was frustrated they were not removed sooner. I gave him his bath and did my usual foot massage and total body care all while I talked and sang to him. His temperature came down for a short time, only to rise again.

I didn't want to go home that evening; I wanted to know who would be taking over his care for the twelve-hour night shift. At about six o'clock, our favorite, Dr. Jones, stepped off the elevator and I let out an audible sigh at the sight of her; she knew Don's history so well and I felt safe with her there. I stopped her and told her what his clinical picture looked like. She did not like what she heard. Within an hour, she had pulled the CVP line and the line for dialysis, which had been there for seven of the eight days. She ordered blood for him, hoping it would expand his volume and raise his blood pressure.

Around nine o'clock, I decided to head home because I had an early morning airport run to take our bonus daughter and grandbaby to the airport. They were scheduled to get home late on Labor Day. Knowing that Dr. Jones was there gave me some measure of comfort, and I was physically and emotionally exhausted. I feared for Don's declining condition and prayed that if he recovered, he'd be brought back to us whole.

Chapter 14

DAY NINE / COLOUR OF MY LOVE

I'll paint my mood in shades of blue, paint my soul to be with you. I'll sketch your lips in shaded tones, draw your mouth to my own. I'll paint the sun to warm your heart swearing that we'll never part. That's the colour of my love."

—Celine Dion

It was Labor Day, September first, and the drop-off at the airport went without incident. I went home for a short nap, waiting out the hospital's morning shift change. Surely someone would have called if he had not been doing well, I thought. I assumed since I hadn't heard anything during the night that everything was okay. I was wrong.

I arrived at the hospital a little before eleven, stopping on the way to get my usual chai soy latte from Starbucks. I parked the car in the North Tower and went right to the Saperstein building. Paul Pape arrived at the same time I did. We hugged and then I went straight to Don's room where he lay very still on the bed. Though he looked peaceful and comfortable, his breathing was different somehow: a breath, then a long pause, and his head would move just a little when he struggled to inhale. His pupils were fixed and dilated. Then I smelled it. It's the smell of death coming: a pungent odor released on each exhale that is something between a mold smell and rancid decay. I began my morning cleanup, washed his face, brushed his teeth, and rubbed his feet, but I knew this was the day I'd say goodbye to my boy—the day he would leave this earthly plane. My heart broke in two, but I wanted to be with him on his way out.

The doctor came in then, looked bleakly at me, and said some words I'll never remember. I knew if anyone could pull out of this, Don would, through his sheer desire to be with us, especially for the girls and his new grandbaby.

Platinum machines hummed in the fluorescent-lit room, coupled with the swishing sounds and the low rhythmic beeping of the heart monitor. IV machines quietly dripped fluids, and the bright lights gave out a high-pitched buzz as they shone down on the perfectly still body of my boy, covered by a starched white sheet. The green wave pattern on the heart-rate monitor showed the slowed but steady activity. *Here is the greatest love I will ever know,* I thought.

For eight days, as I'd stood in this room or dozed in the chair with the noises and beeps, all I could see was hope, but today—day nine—hope was evaporating and I was hit with reality. I went outside the room and asked Paul to please call our pastor, Dr. Keene.

"He's not going to make it," I said.

Then I called my sister, Kathy. I spoke only one word. All I got out was her name.

She simply said, "I'm on my way."

For that moment, I lost my voice. I was overwhelmed at the present reality: I knew I was going to spend the rest of my life without Don. My sweet daughters would have to live without Daddy.

I called my dear friend Adam, and he told me he was on his way, too.

Paul came to me and said, "Nita, we can't give up hope."

"He won't survive this. I know it. I've seen it," was my reply.

I hurried back to Don's bedside to wait for what I knew was coming. Here was my husband, my life partner, and the father of my children about to make his exit from his earthly body. I did not want to miss a millisecond of his remaining life— not even this. "Oh God," I prayed, "Please help me to bear this moment."

I leaned over to kiss him and realized he needed and wanted my permission—
that he'd waited for me to get there that day. I told him it was okay. I knew he was
trying to fight to be here, but his body was tired.

"It's okay to let go, Donnie; I will always love you."

I stood with the tears falling from my eyes, trying to stay present in this awful
moment, softly stroking Don's face and kissing him.

The monitor above showed a rapidly declining heart rate. I moved to the
foot of the bed, rubbing his feet and sang quietly to him. Then I saw it—a white,
translucent puff lifted away from Don's body and disappeared into the air above
him.

I had never seen anything like it. I thought I was tired and I was perhaps seeing
things. I have discovered that we tend to question moments we witness in the
spiritual realm, but I believe I witnessed one that morning.

It was Labor Day, 2008. People everywhere in the US were gathered for
barbecues and dinners, laughing and enjoying life while I stood in an ICU room
losing my husband.

The next few moments were surreal—running in slow motion, out of sync
with time. Like a record playing too slowly, sounds around me were garbled. The
attending physician was in and out of the room because he, too, knew the pattern:
low blood pressure, low heart rate, ventricular fibrillation of the heart, then
asystole: flatline. I was firmly rooted at Don's side, singing into his ear. I had my face
pressed against his, hearing his breaths, spaced farther and farther apart.

"Are we gonna do this, Donnie?" I whispered.

Even in this stark moment, we still made decisions together, that I would let
him go and he would let go too.

The doctor came in and asked what I wanted to do. They had been giving him
every medicine possible to bring up his blood pressure. Nothing was working. But
even then, knowing what I knew, I couldn't let go quite yet. I thought of our girls. I

had to try for the girls. I thought of our life—what I would be bringing Don back to if they could save him.

"Do it," I said to the doctor.

Nurses swooped in with defibrillating paddles to electrically disrupt his heart's fibrillation and help it regain a normal rhythm. The metal paddles were lifted from the crash cart and placed on his chest, one in the center, another on his left side. Then the nurse said, "Clear!"

Don's body lifted and relaxed. His heart's rhythm went into V fibrillation; his blood pressure was seventy over fifty; his breathing agonal with dilated pupils.

"Epi one hundred mg IV push," said the doctor.

Nothing.

Then, rhythmic chest compressions. The rhythm slowed; his pressure continued to drop. They used the paddles a second time, following normal protocol for advanced cardiac life support. Donnie's chest rose a little bit, as did my hope. I just stood at the edge of the room, watching, Paul holding me up on one side.

Pastor Larry walked into the room and moved right past me to get to Don. The doctors said, "Wait," and he came to stand on the other side of me, trying to give me words of comfort. He may have started to pray or speak scriptures gently. I couldn't see or hear anything. I just stared at the heart monitor.

A nurse got on his knees and climbed on one side of the bed to apply the pressure needed for a chest compression in an effort to create a heart rhythm since the defibrillation had not changed his ventricular fibrillation.

Suddenly I heard whimpering and realized the sound was coming from me. Some other guttural noises escaped from my lips; I wanted to scream and run. I still see all of it now, although it was years ago; there I stood, not wanting to believe my eyes and ears.

As an ICU nurse I'd been a part of many of these codes, delivering the chest compressions or pushing the protocol medications. But it is so different when it is happening to a person who is sacred in your heart. So very different. I can see myself just outside his small room, watching this unfold as it was happening, and reliving it again.

I was looking for any heart rhythm other than what I saw on the monitor. I wanted and hoped for a new sign of life, but no sign appeared; his heart rhythm stayed the same.

Meds, chest compressions, a glance at the monitor. Meds, chest compressions, a glance at the monitor. It seemed an eternity as everything moved in slow motion.

For fifteen minutes, the medical team worked to save my boy's life. Then the doctor looked at me and said, "Mrs. LaFontaine, it looks bleak."

I said, "Give me two more minutes . . . for my girls."

And they continued to try and save Don.

Then the moment arrived: I couldn't stand it anymore.

"Please stop. He's not here. Please stop the code." I wanted Don to leave with some measure of dignity. My words stopped all life-saving efforts. The nurse climbed off the side of the bed. Everyone quietly left the room. Some of the nurses cried. Some touched me as they filed out. They "called it," as we say in ICU terms, removing the EKG leads and some IVs. They stopped all the meds and marked that moment in time as his time of death.

Once the respirator was disconnected, I stood, anxiously waiting for them to leave so I could go to Don's side and be with him. When they were gone, I moved close to Don and bent down, my face beside his. The endotracheal tube was still taped to his mouth. There was perhaps one more breath, and then it was done: the one breath that stood between life and death had been breathed.

Paul left to make calls. Pastor Larry was standing on the other side of the bed. I remember feeling so lost in that moment, as if I had just watched my own life end. Then my mind swirled. *How will I be able to move past this moment? What will I say to my girls? How will I tell Christine and her new little boy who Don loved so very much?*

Tremendous uncertainty and overwhelming sadness poured over me. It took me right back to the moments when my mother ascended. I tried to find the words, the strength and the courage to say to my fourteen- and eighteen-year-old girls that Daddy had died, that he had not survived. What do you say, and how do you say it?

This was the moment I lost my voice. There are no words—none that wouldn't be catastrophic for them. I remember what I felt when I was told of my mother's death, and I hoped to be able to hold my girls in a safe space as they came to grips with the news of the loss of their wonderful father.

It was November 1977. I learned of my mother's death by phone during my first semester of college. When I left her to go to back school she was on a respirator and my father insisted that I go back because that was what my mother would want.

We had kept vigil at the hospital for a week, spending our days in the waiting room while she was on a respirator and IVs, her eyes closed. She had suffered a stroke and a heart attack in the hospital during her third peritoneal dialysis.

I went back to school because my father wanted us to have some sense of normalcy. What else was there for me to do that was normal? Ironically, 1977 was the same year Don's only sister died.

The phone call came during a Louisiana thunderstorm: it was dark and rainy, with bolts of lightning as though the skies were weeping buckets. The call was quiet. It was my sister Alene.

"Nita," she said.

I said, "What?"

"You know what."

"No, I need you to tell me."

And then she said, "Mama's gone."

And there was silence and a deep breath, and I said, "Should I come now?"

And she said "We're sending someone for you."

It was a two-hour drive to Monroe and another two to drive back to Shreveport.

I hung up the phone and my roommate, Debra, said, "Was that it?"

I remember having a pink foam roller in my hair for my bangs and as I was taking it out in the bathroom, the tears started to roll down my face. There was no screaming, just the sounds of my tears as they hit the porcelain sink. The last memories I had of my mother were of her in that hospital bed. I didn't have a chance to say goodbye in a quiet way and it was a long time before I could remember her any other way than laying in that bed.

The next time I saw her she was in a casket.

When I arrived at my childhood home, there were cars are all over the place, people falling on me and crying for me. I thought, *Can I just have a freakin' moment to deal with all this?* I was much too polite to say that so I said nothing and ended up consoling them, instead. I couldn't even be sad.

At this juncture of releasing my true love, I leaned on the lesson I learned when I lost my mom: that upon the impact of learning of the loss of a loved one, the best gift to give someone is a little space. Our human instinct is to be ever-present so the grieving one doesn't feel so alone, but a little alone time goes a long way in helping quiet your mind instead of having to be the bereaved hostess or host.

I stood there looking at Don in his stillness, at the end of this magnificent life on earth, and I mustered my voice to say, "I need to be alone with him."

Chapter 15

SAY WHAT YOU NEED TO SAY

*"Even if your hands are shaking and your faith is broken, even as the eyes are closing,
do it with a heart wide open, say what you need to say."*

—John Mayer

Standing in the still, odd silence of that square, florescent-lit room, I was without words. I was without everything in that moment. I couldn't feel my heart. I just looked at him and looked at him, and the tears rolled. Screams without sounds were buried inside my being. My insides were wild and primal and had I followed those instincts, I think I would have run until I hit a wall. There was so much anguish, tightness, fear, rage, unbelievable sadness, and grief for my children snowballing in my chest, yet I touched him and hoped that, like in the fairy tales, my love, tears, or kisses would bring him back to perfect life. He didn't come back, but the reality didn't hit me, either.

They left me and Don alone for some time, then Dr. Kimchi appeared and stood beside me. He gently spoke of what a great man Don was. He was heartbroken to lose a dear friend and patient. I felt his loss but was frozen in my own pain and disbelief.

For eight days, all I saw was hope. We knew people who had survived terrible things and I planned on our joining that exclusive club. Walking into his room on September first, I knew it was the last time I would see him here, wash his body, read him a page from a book or newspaper over the dull hiss-pahh of the respirator and the clicks of the IV machines, or tell him how well Obama was doing and how great his speech was at the Democratic National Convention. And now . . .

My next thoughts were for my children. *What will I say to them? How will we survive without their Dad?* Even now thinking of that moment brings me to tears. I heard someone say after losing their spouse that they expected to feel sad but they didn't expect to feel afraid. That was my experience. I did not know our lives without him. I couldn't imagine it, nor did I want to. How would I parent the girls as a single, widowed mother? How could we feel happy? How would I be the voice for both of us?

Our lives had been one motion, one word, "DonandNita," dancing and singing as a team. How could I dance without my partner, my confidant, my best friend, my love? The anxiety and uncertainty of all these things robbed me for a time of my voice, and since I didn't have his to lean on or to comfort me, I was silent, praying in my head, trying to figure it all out.

Our friends started arriving as word quickly spread. I asked someone to please not let the girls watch TV until I could get to them. They were at a friend's home trying to enjoy some part of the holiday and perhaps laugh a little. What was there to say? He's gone? I don't want to be here without him? What will our lives be like without him? How will we manage?

It was time to leave after an hour or so of hugging, crying, and seeing the faces of friends who loved him coming there to be a support for me—for us. I was surrounded by family and friends who shielded me. Deb, Adam, Pastor Larry and Virginia, and Paul were all there. They wanted to drive me home, but I needed to be with myself and take in what had transpired, and mostly to pray for the right words and the right way to summon the courage and strength to use my somber, lifeless voice for our young daughters, who would be receiving the most devastating news of their young lives.

As I got onto the fifth floor elevator of Saberstein Tower at Cedars, I looked back at the waiting room that had held so many loved ones for nine days, and all that had transpired there: the loving visitors, the core family group that had been there day in and day out, and the hope we held onto through the ordeal. I would never again walk the hallway leading to the ICU where Don was.

I pushed the elevator button for the first floor. Paul, Pastor Larry and Virginia, and Deb rode with me, but I was speechless. The newness and pain of this moment is inexplicable. The thought heaviest on my heart was my daughters—having to tell them, and having to create a new reality for them. My brain felt like a fuzzy screen on the television. There was sound and noise, but nothing that made sense.

We reached the first floor and started to go through the sliding glass door leading out of the building. For a moment, my feet felt nailed to the floor but I stepped off the elevator and again looked around at my altered universe. This was the last barrier between Don and me; I was leaving him there, never to come again to see him, hug him, and kiss his face. It was more than I could bear. My spirit cried out, "God help me!" because at that moment I couldn't see my way at all. I knew I had to get to my girls; I didn't want them to learn about their daddy's death any way other than from me.

Stepping out of the downstairs elevator on the first floor of Cedars-Sinai Hospital's Saperstein Tower I began the most difficult walk of my life, through those sliding glass doors and out of the looming building into the sunlight. It felt like the world should pause. Didn't they know I'd just left the love of my life for the last time? Couldn't they tell by my sad posture and tear-stained face? Everything looked the same, but warped and out of time. People couldn't possibly bustle around me when I had just lost my husband. How could they talk and laugh? How could the sun come out today?

I heard someone say the news of Don's passing had leaked and was hitting the airways—before we left the hospital! That snapped me back to reality. I put one foot in front of the other and with the help of my loved ones, crossed the threshold between what was and what was to be. It was the hardest step I've ever had to take so far. I intuitively knew that I was forever changed, not by death, but by love. A great love that spanned twenty-two years, two beautiful daughters, much laughter, mischief, adventures, and wonderful travels: a grand life of love together. I drove home in silence and prayer.

Chapter 16

ONE MOMENT IN TIME

"Give me one moment in time when I'm more than I thought I could be.
One moment when I'm racing with destiny."

——Whitney Houston

The next few days and moments were so painful it took all the strength I've ever had just to speak with my baby girls. The outpouring from the community at large that loved, respected, and cherished this great man was a like a rain shower in the midst of my life firestorm. Don's website received nearly eight million hits as the news spread. The news of his passing scrolled across the TV during the Republican convention. I knew he was loved but I had no idea the scope and reach of his voice in the world. The emails, food, calls, cards, and flowers were in overabundance. It truly was a miracle to feel all these angels around me holding us up with their prayers and their presence.

My family had worked in the funeral home business (my father was a co-owner at one time), so they knew what needed to be done. They called the biggest and most well-known cemetery in town for me, and were informed they were so busy they could not "pick up" his body for two weeks. Can you believe that? I called a couple others but there must have been a two-for-one sale on death because there was no one available to get my boy from the hospital. (Okay, that's a bad joke.)

My sister mentioned a place called Hollywood Forever Cemetery. I giggled, thinking she was making a joke, only to find out it was real place, and that one of Don's idols, Mel Blanc, was also buried there. The name was perfect because Don was "Mr. Hollywood."

They were able to pick him up from the hospital right away. My sisters were handling all of this because I was overwhelmed. The location seemed ideal, just behind Paramount Movie Studios, where he once worked as vice president of advertising. So this would be the place chosen for us, after nearly being unable to find one. Of course it was the perfect resting place: there are no coincidences.

Our home was and always has been a haven. Our girls' friends and cousins slept over and cried with them, just wanting to be near them for support. Christine and her then-fiancé stayed in the privacy of the well-appointed lower level of the house. It was hard for her, I know. She had had the most years with him.

One night Liisi came into my room from down the hall and said, "Mommy, can you help us?"

I came into the guest room where she and three friends were getting ready to go to sleep. They were stuck in a sad place and couldn't stop crying—for Liisi and some for themselves, I supposed. Don had been a part of their lives: he had driven with them and been a father figure to them as well.

I prayed for guidance to give them words that could help. I reminded them first that it was okay to cry and feel sad. Then I reminded them of something Don had said or done that made them laugh, so they could remember all the fun they'd had with him. They began to tell Don stories as I knelt on the floor beside them and some of those tears slowly became giggles after a while. This was one of many times that the fun of Don's love and light made me giggle and feel warm, and them too. As I relayed this to the children, I also said it to myself.

I struggled with each decision. Choosing the casket was the hardest and landed me on my knees many times. There was a room at the funeral home with several choices and just walking into it pierced my heart like a knife. Ann Walker Susskind was right there with us. She had gone through this five years ago when her husband Steve—Don's best friend—was killed in a car accident on a sunny day.

One casket was really outstanding and kept winking at me. It was the shiniest, prettiest, most expensive thing in the room. After looking at them all, I chose it for

Don. He always loved a fancy car and I wanted him to ride out in style just as he had in life.

Choosing the plot was equally difficult. These were all the things we should have done beforehand but we simply were too busy living to plan on dying anytime soon.

The funeral was an intimate gathering of three hundred close beloved friends and family. The hearse was late arriving and the limo with the girls, me, and my niece had to wait until they had entered before we could arrive. I was spared seeing my father break down as the casket was rolled into the sanctuary for Don's memorial service. I felt like I'd been punched in the gut at the sight of it but I couldn't fall because my girls needed me today more than ever. I laid my hand on the casket for balance, though I thought I would faint and I really wanted to wail and scream at this moment, but my girls are watching and holding their breath for me and for themselves.

His sisters' sons, five of them, had flown in from Minnesota. I could look no farther than their direction, where they sat with heads bowed in grief and broken-heartedness.

Charles Randolph Wright (Don's other heart brother, born on the same day, and godfather to Liisi), Paul, my sisters Kathy and Alene, and Pastor Larry—who'd performed thousands of these services—had a big hand in helping us.

Charles began the service by reading a scripture. He shared with me later that he'd come to visit Don a couple weeks before he passed, and Don said, "I want you to take care of my girls."

Charles said later that he didn't take it in fully at the time and brushed it off as frustrated talk. As Virgos, they knew each other's rhythms, had a sense of order and cleanliness, and no one rooted for Charles or celebrated his accomplishments more than Don. These words were what drove Charles's heart in the days after Don's passing, and he bravely stepped up to be a strong male figure in my girls' lives.

I remember it just as it was. My cousin, Dr. Carl Whitaker from Chattanooga, prayed a meaningful prayer. Then our friend Wil Wheaton sang the song he'd sung at our wedding: "Ferris Wheel." Virginia, Pastor Larry's wife, sang, too. It was a loving, moving service; filled with music, fond memories, and great Don stories from family, colleagues, and friends.

Don's time in the Army had made him quite patriotic. My sister found and read a beautiful explanation of why the flag was folded as my cousin and thirty-year Navy veteran Edward folded the flag.

Paul found a recording of Don's voice reciting the *Pledge of Allegiance;* we played it after the folding to end that section of the program. Everyone broke into applause as Don's voice boomed those words complete with a musical underscore. There was an audible, collective gasp when we voice first came into the room. It was a moving and exhilarating moment to hear his voice filling the room, filling our hearts for that glorious moment. Love gathers people, and even though the occasion was somber, Don's loving voice brought us joy in that moment and our love for him was united. Our friend Ben teased, "God wanted His voice back!"

Don's dear friend Dr. Asher Kimchi eloquently summed up some of what Don meant to us all:

Dear Family and friends,

For millions of people around the world, Don LaFontaine was recognized as the "Voice of God." For me he was the voice of a close and dear friend.

We first met on May 5, 1989, exactly nineteen years and four month ago, when he came to my cardiology office for a treadmill stress test. For all those who knew him it will be easy to understand that it would not take more than a few minutes to realize that you have just met a unique and special person. He was smart, witty, had a charming personality, that radiated far, and his caring and compassion to others became obvious very quickly.

Don was one of those people, that, when you meet him, you hoped to see him again soon and you wish that he will continue to be part of your life.

Luckily the bond between us was formed very quickly, we were able to share with each other our feelings, thoughts and experiences. He was sensitive and always eager to listen and help.

Don LaFontaine was the voice of a good mentor. He took upon himself the role of teaching and helping other young professionals to advance their career in the voice acting and movie trailer business. He guided many of his peers, either personally or through interviews, writing and publications.

Don LaFontaine was the voice of humility.

Despite his tremendous accomplishments he rarely emphasized them or put them at the center of his conversations. Our conversations would cover many different topics but he would rarely touch on his glorious career.

For me Don LaFontaine was the voice of a philanthropic person, he gave much of himself for good causes, in particular if they had to do with children. He would volunteer and offer his talent and voice, as the voice of G-d for fundraising events and supported Nita when she was performing and singing in galas or nonprofit organizations events.

Don LaFontaine was the voice of a proud father. He was blessed with having three gorgeous and beautiful daughters and a grandson. They were his pride and joy. Many times, without asking, he would reach to his back pocket, grab his wallet, open it and show me photos of his lovely daughters. I could tell by the excitement and his shiny eyes how happy he was and how much they topped everything else in his life.

Don was also the voice of a loving and caring husband. For Don, Nita was a present from heaven that he cherished and enjoyed every single moment. He was proud of her as a mother, as a nurse, and as a performing artist. He always made sure to tell Becky, my wife, and me about the advancement in her career, to inform us about her future and upcoming concerts and was very happy to see us celebrating her performances with them.

In a world where a new and true friendship is not easily found, Don LaFontaine was a close and dear friend of all of us here. His love and friendship will stay with all of us forever.

May G-d bless us all.

I had not planned to speak at the service; I didn't think I could. We had crafted a beautiful service filled with his light and our dearest family and friends to remember Don and all his brilliance and love. But the morning of the memorial service, some words poured out of me as soon as I woke; I knew I had to share them, to tell our story more intimately.

I went to my computer to jot down those thoughts and it came quickly in about five minutes, what I wanted to say about us. I was finding my voice, and I knew that I needed to say something about what our love was like. When we had arrived at the service, Pastor Larry greeted us at the back door to receive us and I whispered to him, "I want to say something."

The piece of paper was folded four times to fit in the small black purse I carried. My cell phone and tissues were its only companions. There is a legal document called advanced directive that gives a person of your choosing the right to speak for you in the event you cannot do it for yourself; essentially, that person is to be your voice, usually in the case of severe sickness or death. Don had given me that role and I had given it to him for me. It was not easy, because in the midst of trying to honor what Don would have wanted, I was so broken and vulnerable that my thinking wasn't always as clear as I thought it would be, and I felt torn.

Standing before loved ones, I knew I had to be the voice for our love, what we were, and what we would always be to each other. This is not a verbatim recall, but I remember telling them I met Don as a medallion-wearing, Jaguar-driving, blow-dryer-haired man who surprised me by becoming the prince of my dreams; that our only difference was that I was tall and he was short. I think our love surprised him, too, because neither of us was looking for each other. I said Don's picture should be in the dictionary under the word "love" and that I'd never known a more generous person of self and spirit than he. I said Don was a thinker ahead of his time and that he would set the standard for everyone else to follow, including the limo he'd insisted on using, and his home studio.

I tried to convey all the things we were, and how fantastic, pure, and perfect was our love; that he was the love of my life and a once-in-a-lifetime love, destined to travel together for a time on this plane, and continuing to dance together for an eternity through our hearts.

I said he'd set a gold standard in the voice-over business—a template and a standard for others in the way he lived his life: fully with intention in each day and integrity that was noble and honorable. A saint he was not, but he was perfect for me, I said.

I think I ended with words I still can barely write or say: "Goodnight, my Prince." I thought my heart would break in that moment and my knees could not hold the weight of my broken heart and spirit.

Pastor Larry Keene lifted us higher with his inspired words and eulogy in "The Lord's Prayer." It was so beautiful he nearly converted every Jewish person in the room. As we left, I saw concerned, sad, and tear-stained faces trying to connect with mine, but it was too much and I rushed to the limo.

There I saw Don's housekeeper, Connie, and her daughter crying. I hugged them before getting into the car. I was moved beyond tears by the love that filled that room in honor of a great man and a great life.

We had arranged for an outdoor gathering at another part of the cemetery that had an open grassy area; I couldn't bear having all those people at our home, which was bursting at the seams already. As we approached his place of resting, people began to get out of their cars and walk toward the gathering place.

I was focused on trying to be present for my daughters, all three. They are all the best parts of him. Christine was never very talkative, but she has the same wit, blue eyes, and love of reading as her dad. Skye is stoic and always sees the good in everything; she is kind, smart, and talented with a great thirst for books, a beautiful smile, and looks very much like her Dad; she is like a breath of fresh air. Liisi has a groundedness and old-soul aura about her. She is bright, sensitive, quite expressive, and always speaks her mind. She helped me make the crucial decisions I could not make in the whirlwind of activity. She asked me not to lower the casket.

As I stood on the grass and dirt beside a silver Cadillac casket holding the remains of the love of my life, I was handed a white dove by a gentleman who explained how doves always find their way home, and the metaphor of our souls finding their way home. Holding the dove, I felt its heart beating in my hands as it wiggled to be free. I could feel his wings pushing against my closed hands as I clutched them around his fat fluffy middle, trying to break free. The moment I opened my hands he flew toward the sky with such grace and ease that I could feel a swoosh and an exhale as though Don were saying, "I'm breathing now, honey . . . I'm free. No chains of illness can bind me now."

And with each dove that flew from the hands of each daughter toward the fluffy cloud-dotted blue sky, I knew this was the gift of the dove: to remind me of the freedom in the sky and the quiet of the wind as its wings expanded white and graceful and singing through the air that would become the angel wings watching over me in moments when I could no longer see them. This was the gift of that moment that I shall never forget; that those wings flapping gracefully and free symbolized the wings that would be Don's to comfort and protect us. How am I standing in this moment, this unreality that hasn't really hit me yet? My two teenaged daughters and my older bonus daughter stood there in silence with tear tracks streaking their faces. I could barely embrace the pain and inexplicable joy of the moment: the joy of Don being released from sickness, and the pain of the loss of my prince and life partner and the father of my children.

Chapter 17

CELEBRATE GOOD TIMES

*"Celebrate good times, come on! So bring your good times
and your laughter too, we gonna celebrate your party with you!"*

———Kool and the Gang

Knowing many relatives who'd flown in could not afford to come back and forth
to Los Angeles, we planned a celebration of Don's life event, commemorating a life
well lived. Dress: Circus attire!

When Don was a boy of twelve or so, he and his sister won a few dance
competitions. The movies of his childhood era influenced him greatly and he
adopted that flair in his adult life, loving to dress with style when he wasn't driving
carpool. He wore the collar turned up on his leather jackets like James Dean, and
he loved the style and class of Bogart, Grant, James Stewart, and Rock Hudson. A
romantic, irreverent, old school gentleman, he loved an opportunity to pull out his
white suit with foulard and matching tie to go out with his taller wife. We had to
celebrate his life in a way that involved dressing up and having fun.

We wanted to create a joyful celebration to honor his life. Don always felt that
life was a big party to be enjoyed, celebrated, and reveled in. True to that style, we
wanted to imbue this evening with all those elements that reflected the grandiose
way Don lived his life, helping the rest of us to live more fully. Everyone was
dressed to the nines.

The emails, food, flowers, and love continued to flow in abundance as we
planned for Don's special celebration day. Though often overwhelming, for the first
time I began to understand the reach and scope of Don's voice in the world. Not

only those who knew him personally, but people who'd had only passing contact with him were deeply saddened by his passing, and a rain of condolences poured in.

I had some idea that Don was at the top of his voice-over game, but the emails, cards, and calls that came in helped me to see that his voice was loved around the world, not just among the Los Angeles voice-over community. He was given credit for being the Screen Actors Guild busiest working actor because of the sheer number of contracts he had signed. The voice-over community proclaimed him the template through which all voice-over announcers learned their delivery. Some said he grandfathered the art of voice-over. But more than all that, the stories came out about how Don reached out to, mentored, and taught others. The generosity of his spirit and the gift of his time to so many manifested as an indelible mark he left on so many.

Adam Jackson, my brothah from anothah mothah, pulled together a choir of great voices we lovingly called "The United Voices of LaFontaine" to help us prepare for Don's celebration day. Charles, Paul, and Kathy were involved and each took a task so that we could pull all the pieces together to make it truly a "Show" of love for our beloved boy. The celebration was inspiring, joyful, and laughter-filled, leaving our hearts fuller for having known him and having gathered in that place. It was exactly as he would have wanted.

Takeo drummers opened the celebration, a regal call befitting the prince of a man Don was, and he'd loved their majestic sound. They were followed by a comical video that made the audience roar with laughter. People dressed in their best colors; I wore gold because my husband treated me like a goddess.

The United Voices of LaFontaine sang beautifully, followed by several endearing Don stories. People spoke of Don's generosity of spirit and kindness, voice-over artists spoke about his mentoring, teaching, and generous spirit that spilled over into their lives and professions, and I spoke about the center of his being: his unconditional love for his family and fellow man, not forgetting his eccentricity and irreverence, made him a beautiful dichotomy (as brilliant as he was, he was equal parts prankish and silly) as well as a pioneer in the field of voice-over—not only because of the volume and body of his work, but because of how he laid the groundwork for the art form itself for so many to follow.

One announcer gave an example of Don's eccentricity. He told a story about a time when he ordered caviar with Don after a New York meeting, and the announcer said, "That is so expensive!" Don, wanting to encourage them to try something new and extravagant, replied, "Hey guys, it's a spot and a tag." In voice-over lingo, that meant it was a quick session tag. The words, "Coming tonight on NBC" at the studio would pay for it in seconds. In other words, "Live a little!"

He always had a quick joke, and could get me every time he faked walking into a door. Don's love of laughter was infectious and we all caught the bug when we were around him. But, when he would drop into the voice-over booth and almost always give a one-take performance, ever the consummate professional.

Every one of the eight hundred or so people who squeezed into the celebration left wanting to be better people. Finally, our friend David Foster played a haunting piano melody he'd played once with Don. At the end of the piece, he invited us all to stand and give Don a standing ovation. The thunderous sound nearly lifted the roof from the building. I felt Don's presence very strongly that night and felt as though he was surprised by all the fuss about him, yet he loved it and was slightly amused by it all.

Broderick Miller, director of the kids' theater group, ended the ceremony with these words:

"We were all privileged to celebrate Don's life through video/audio clips and the moving remembrances of family and friends. We learned more about Don's decency, integrity, honesty, generosity, loyalty, and enormous sense of humor than we could have possibly known. Something happened Tuesday night, and I think it snuck up on all of us. We said goodbye to a larger-than-life force of talent and kindness, but we also were given a gift. We were given a powerful example and inspiration to be better in our own

lives: better friends, better fathers, better husbands, better mentors, and better human beings. Thank you, Don, for impacting us in this very meaningful way."

I couldn't have said it better myself.

Chapter 18

BACK TO LIFE

"Back to life, back to reality."

—Soul II Soul

My core family stayed with me for a week after the celebration to help me begin to piece together all the parts of my life and give me direction. I was utterly lost, though I went to meetings and performed other perfunctory tasks. When the crowds of people returned to their lives, I was left with the stark reality of the new normal in my life. When Death comes, it is everywhere; it's in your room, in your house, and in your thoughts. I kept replaying the day Don died over and over again in my head trying to figure out if there was something else we could have done differently. The idea that this person I loved so very deeply was gone from this earth—that I wasn't going to see his eyes or kiss his mouth or hold him—was deeply unsettling and sometimes more than I thought I could bear. It is only now that I see how grace began to show itself as a quiet guide on this new road through my saddest moments and realizations.

When I looked at my children, I gained strength from them. I knew that if I went into that black hole of sadness, I might not return. Then who would shepherd my children? I somehow understood right away that it was important I keep everything else in their lives as normal as possible. I signed Liisi up for dance classes and enrolled her on the school volleyball team. Being physical and hitting a ball hard could be therapy for her and an outlet. Skye had a full schedule as it was her senior year and she would be applying to colleges and all that entailed. They both signed up again to be a part of a theater group, which was another great outlet and a second home for them.

My new routine was not a routine at all. I took my daughter to school and sat in a parking lot and cried. Or drove around crying, before calling my Dad or my sister or Adam or Deb. I didn't want to go home; I wasn't sure how to fill my days yet, though there was so much to do. There was always something to do when Don was there. Now there was a void and time on my hands that I had not yet learned to use productively. I am sure there were things that needed doing, but I just ignored them. Not wanting to feel the new emptiness of my home; I avoided it.

My dad talked me through the first minutes when I felt my sadness would burst through my chest, then I cried more and drove aimlessly, not knowing where I was going, but ultimately ending up at back home: at my new reality, my new life. The dogs' loudly barked greetings and unconditional love eased me back into the house. It was a light, moment-to-moment tread as grief was my constant companion and the confusion of the new normal kept my head barely above the water line of life.

I was also very concerned with how the girls were expressing their grief when they were away from me. This consumed my thoughts because I wanted to be there quickly if they began to fall apart. I cleared my calendar and was ready at a moment's notice to be with them if they needed me.

Reading the grief pamphlets given to me at the hospital and speaking with a counselor at Our House (a grief support group), I learned that kids grieve differently than adults. So I watched and listened to them, and never took their Dad out of our conversations. Liisi needed to sleep in Daddy's place, and Skye needed her alone time. She would bring up many funny stories about her dad, but didn't cry a lot in my presence. Liisi wore a necklace that he'd worn recently and instinctively began to write down things he'd said. She simply would say, "I don't want to forget what Daddy used to say." I reassured her she wouldn't, but this was part of the way she coped. She wanted and needed her Daddy's voice, his words to be inked somewhere for later times when the memories wouldn't be as clear. His voice and arms had always been a safe place for her—for them both—and I hoped the memory of them could continue to be. When I saw my girls trying to hold on to the precious memories of their dad; my heart broke for them.

My father understood all too well what I was going through, and his other advice to me was, "Just keep getting up. I know it's hard baby girl, but you're gonna make it. If you are brought to it, the Grace of God will see you through it."

How elevating is that? I kept getting up, even though I wanted to live under the covers, stay in my room, and sit in the pool of sorrow and pity surrounding me. *But my children need me.* And I needed me, too; I didn't want to lose my life and myself to this overwhelming grief. Though it stopped me in my tracks and crashed like tsunami waves over me, I kept getting up—if only physically—and his encouragement helped me to do that, to keep going. *Thank you Daddy for such wise words.*

My mother's sister, sweet Aunt Lillian, stayed with me for several weeks, steady as a rock to just be there until I could get a grip on finding a new rhythm in my life and to cook for us. What a lovely gift she gave.

Getting back to life wasn't easy by any means. We struggled to grasp it. My dad told me it was important for the girls to get back to some sense of normalcy, which was what he had done with us after our mother had died. So after two weeks, I sent the girls back to their schools. They'd missed the critical first two weeks, but so what. Not knowing this new road, I did know that what had happened to them was catastrophic. They were still in shock, but sitting around the house wasn't helping anyone, especially them. Being back in the environment of their peers would be a distraction more than anything, and a way for them to connect to the world outside the hole we were living in. The adjustment was subtle and loud, big and small—

the wanting to call Dad to ask for a word, a rhyme, his opinion on a project, his thoughts on a subject, and not seeing him at his place for dinner were the moments that could take the life from their lives and the sadness of it all would sit on them like a boulder.

I protected their tender state in conferences with teachers and principals who thought only of the work they'd missed. I told them, "We're not catching up. You're just going to have to start where they are." They were all sympathetic and a couple teachers kept a mother's eye on my girls. I knew I would speak the words they didn't know how to speak for themselves. From the whispers at Don's bedside to this moment, my voice was becoming stronger. I am and always will be Skye and Liisi's mother. I also let their teachers and counselors know they would be engaging their school peers, getting out of the house and back to their lives. The advice of my brilliant therapist Penelope Jeffries early on was, "Be on the side of your children." That has always stayed with me and that is what Don and I had always done as a team. Now I would do it alone.

Chapter 19

BYE AND BYE

"Bye and bye when the morning comes, All the saints of God are gathering home. We will tell the story of how we've overcome and we'll understand it better bye and bye."

———————————

—Charles A. Tilley

So many people were concerned and worried about how the girls and I were evolving emotionally, but I couldn't speak to everybody; it was simply too much. I couldn't possibly repeat my story over and over. Repeating the story inflamed my sadness and kept me at Don's bedside when I was trying to accomplish the difficult task of beginning my life without him. From the first email I'd sent, rallying prayers when Don became so ill, I discovered emailing was a great way to reach out and talk to our concerned friends and family. I used that medium to reach a mass of people without so many direct phone calls.

After being overwhelmed in general with the details of planning services, seventeen house guests, people dropping by to give us hugs and well wishes, and watching my children carefully, it occurred to me that I could speak to everyone through my writing. I referred to the recipients of my emails as my Prayer Village: those who continued to cover us with their sacred prayers. I also sent emails of gratitude to people who continued to keep us and hold us through the many difficult "firsts." I also was able to articulate things I remembered that I wanted to say at the memorial and the celebration. This is one of the first check-ins that I sent:

Date: Tuesday, September 16, 2008, 12:58 AM

To all of you who love Don,

There is so much I wanted to say at his celebration and didn't. Even If you did not attend, let me first start by saying THANK YOU for the cards, the calls, the FOOD.... THE FOOD, the text messages, the e-mails, flowers, the love and concern you've shown over the past two weeks. It is difficult for me to conceive that it's been two weeks today that Don's soul ascended. Wow. We still feel so sad and lost, like we're on some new planet with familiar things that seem strange somehow. It's like a déjá vu with a big element missing. Thank you for your presence in attending the services honoring Don or for showing up just to hang out with Skye and Liisi.

I wanted to say how much I loved him and how he rocked my world with how he loved me. Endless love was what we felt and the "Nearness of You" was our favorite song for each other. We prayed for a baby on our first anniversary and got two healthy ones who now have his wings to fly on but still feel shaky right now. I wanted to say that Don was born to be a caretaker because he spent most of his youth with his sister's hand in his as his loving mother worked shifts as a waitress and single mother in the '40s; that was a huge part of his being was shaped in his childhood. What a gift.

I wanted to say that there are two types of people, river and reservoir. The Reservoir people get their blessings and keep them close only sharing them with a few that are close. River people get their blessings and let them flow downstream to whomever needs them; Don was a big river person, no doubt. I want to be a river people. I wanted to say how happy and peaceful our home has been and how it so often rang with laughter and song. I wanted to say that he was not perfect but he was perfect for me. No one had a kinder heart and more giving spirit. His intelligence was beyond amazing; he was so well read, he could converse on any subject.

He would have been amazed and pleased I'm sure.

I wanted to say that being busy helps us get through the day but the nights are the worst. That moments sneak up and bring me to tears daily and I pray for strength to be what my children need me to be right now. I pray that their teachers will be more than understanding as the girls find their way into a new normal and rhythm.

I know that so many of you are praying for us and it is helping us and carrying up through these days and the nights.

I wanted to say that I hope you will celebrate Don with me each day by some random act of kindness. That you will speak his name and remember how funny and irreverent he could be yet so loving and sincere.

I wanted to say that I don't know how I am or what I need or how you can help except to check in on those "firsts." The first Christmas, birthday, graduation, concert or recital, without him there.

I wanted to say that if I don't call you back, please don't take it personally; I am just trying to be here and be sane. Many of you have walked this road ahead of me, but this is a place I wish for none of you but if you have to get here, and most will, I pray that you will be guided by the light of love from so many as you have been for the girls and me. I am humbled and grateful for your love and concern. It will be a road but we are still a family, a family standing in the winds and on the wings of a Godly man with a voice from Heaven and a heart of an angel.

If you listen you can hear his voice . . . For all of us who loved him and knew him, there will never be another. Never another voice like his. Never another heart like his, so pure and giving. He was and always will be my prince. We were all proud to have known him. Keep us in your prayers.

He was simply the best.

Gratitude and peace.

This email summed up my feelings of loss in those early weeks. The responses to these emails fortified my resolve to move forward and also helped our "love village" understand where we were on our journey. Writing these emails became my therapeutic place of expression and a way to connect us all; we became a collective community with the singular focus to empower and pray for each other. As much of an outlet as it was for me, it was a window and a bell for people to see and hear how to help us and how to pray for us.

Don and I know that doing something for someone else is the best way to help yourself and the benefit is always a blessing to you. Following this maxim is one of the many elements that made our life together so rich; we were in sync in this practice even before we fell in love, and realized reaching out to others was a common denominator between us. We practiced this ideal throughout our life together and now I would employ this again in the form of my emails messages. In sharing the girls' and my personal journey with those who had been praying for and with us, I was indeed helping myself, but in return I gave the people who care about us assurances that we were surviving our mortal wound. Carrying this forward was something I knew then and know now also kept me out of the hole of depression.

So many had been praying for us while Don was sick and continued those prayers as we began our road through loss to glimmers of healing, that I thought it was important we pray for others as well. I knew I wasn't the only one walking a difficult road or in need of prayer. But even so, in the early weeks, I wrestled with trying not to dwell on the regrets and the what-ifs.

My journey of healing began through these email check-ins, which eventually became into a prayer village where we shared our concerns and prayer needs. Eventually it became a cyberspace to share not only prayer needs but praise reports. Don would have wanted us to share good news and laughter, too. That's so Donnie.

Chapter 20

ON THE WINGS OF LOVE

"On the wings of love, up and above the clouds
the only way to fly is on the wings of love."

—Jeffery Osborne

At night I envisioned Don's enormous wings wrapped around me like a constant hug and force field keeping me safe. Each day I envisioned them as the floor I walked on; I felt as though I was being carried. I knew that I was; I felt his presence but longed to see his face.

Wrung out and exhausted for months, I was unable to read or watch TV. I fell into bed each night and said a simple prayer: "Thank you for this day, dear God, and please give me the strength to take care of my family. Bless us and keep us. Amen."

This prayer guided me and gave me strength to get through the night so I could make it through the next day. The emotions during this time were physically exhausting.

Sometimes my daughters would sleep on either side of me in our bed, creating a mommy sandwich. Sometimes I would wake from the heat of their bodies, but I was happy to have them within arms' reach on those nights.

Shortly after Don's death, I faced my first singing engagement. It had been booked a couple of months before, as I was a cast member of *Once on this Island* for Reprise Theater group. The evening was a talkback—an event at which a theater celebrity is interviewed and shares events from their career with Ben Vereen at the Freud Theater, with Charles R. Wright moderating. I knew I would be among dear friends. I remember telling my dad I didn't think I could do it.

He said, "You should do it. Singin'll make you feel a little better. Don't worry, the Lord will be with you."

I don't recall much of the event leading up to my singing; not driving there or walking into the theater or who was with me (though I know now I was accompanied by my father, brother, and dear friend Clinton).

At some point I realized I had to go somewhere else within myself if I was to get through the song. When I opened my mouth to sing "The Impossible Dream," the words flew out of me with little effort, as though I were simply a vessel or channel for the song to come through. I remember looking to my left and noticing Ben and Charles crying.

Even though I was still emotionally numb and in many parts of my life I was just "going through the motions," I remember feeling that Don was with me. I know the only way I got through my song was because I could feel Don that night. He had always been my greatest fan, yet my sharpest critic. He was always proud of me, and that did make me feel better in that moment.

I am so grateful now that I kept the vision of Don's wings wrapped around me in my mind and my heart. It brought me not only comfort, but these angel-thoughts of my prince boy got me through this first hurdle on my journey through grief.

Later, people who knew of Don came backstage to say hello to Ben. They told me they were in awe of my strength. I simply responded, "I am standing on Don's wings . . . his wings of love."

Chapter 21

NOT A DAY GOES BY

*"Not a day goes by not a single day / But you're somewhere a part of my life /
And it looks like you'll stay / As the days go by / I keep thinking when does it end /
Where's the day I'll have started forgetting?"*

——Steven Sondheim

I remember the many difficult moments, and they are as real when I think about them as they were when I went through them. I still see myself when I was on the dark path of grief.

I see the times when I cry quietly in my bedroom so the girls won't hear me. Several times in public I come undone; I am filling out an application for Liisi's new dance class and there is a space to put the father's occupation. I didn't know what to put. Don was still her father but I thought *He's not doing voice-over anymore* and I could not write "deceased." I fall apart. On another occasion, I was running a simple errand, buying a backpack, I see a tee shirt that reads: "Old guys do it better." I walk to the tee shirt and take it down ready to buy it for Don thinking what a kick and a laugh he'll get out of it before I realize my mistake and run out of the store.

Joan Didion speaks of "magical thinking" in her book: a coping trick your mind can play, when for a few moments you forget your loved one is no longer on earth.

I run to my car and when I can catch my breath, I call my father and tell him I don't know how I'm going to make it.

"Just hold on baby; you're going to be all right," he says, "You're gonna make it. I made it, and you will, too. I know it's hard. God will see you through this, just keep on praying."

Going to the social security office (as I was instructed to do), I lose it talking with the lady there, a complete stranger. Having to talk about him, the recent sting of the loss bubbles up and over.

I was instructed by our attorneys to order death certificates from various agencies that need them (all of this is foreign to me) and I go to pick them up from the funeral director's office. They look surprisingly like birth certificates. I am stunned by an incredible sadness. I stare and stare at the small stack of papers and the tears begin to roll.

All I can say is, "Is this it? Is this what his life is . . . on this paper?"

The paper is blue, and at first glance you would think it was a certificate of life. It felt so strange that an entire life is summed up on a page that is mostly about how that life ended. It doesn't say how they lived or who they loved, what they left behind when they went ahead, how a piece of your heart died with them, how there is a gaping hole in your life that you have no idea how to fill, how the world will miss his voice announcing movies, how much he helped create an art form, how his daughters wouldn't have their father see them graduate high school, get married, or have their babies.

It doesn't say he was a great man or a supreme being who mentored, helped, and gave at every opportunity he could find; it's just sterile piece of sky blue paper with dark blue borders framing typed words on lines filled in by some unknown person who didn't know a thing about him. And with that thought, I lose it again.

He is in my every thought. The *what-ifs, woulda-coulda-shouldas* come up, and I try to figure out how we could have had a different outcome. My mind won't be still or quiet, and won't let me rest. I go to visit the cemetery. Sitting next to his gravesite is so incredibly sad that it weighs on me like a stone. I wear this weight on my shoulders for the rest of that day. *I should not be sitting at the grave of my wonderful husband,* I think. Yet I see the sadness in my girls' eyes as they and I try to get back into a groove of what looks like normal but is, in fact, so far from it.

Preparing to go to Christine's wedding in Pennsylvania that October gave us something to look forward to. Buying the dresses and shoes was a nice distraction for the moment. After returning from her wedding, I sent another check-in email to journal our progress.

October 23, 2008:

Hello to my prayer angels and loved ones,

Don's eldest daughter Christine just got married this weekend! Yeah! She was a lovely bride and I felt Don would have been pleased. It was held in Solebury, Pennsylvania, a lovely town north of Philly. The wedding was a bit chilly (outdoors for a brisk 47 degree, 15 minute ceremony...) but the colors of fall on the east coast are one of God's canvases that are always illuminating. Seeing little Riley (the grandbaby) with that gap in his front teeth, reminded me of Don's baby pictures! He is a very cute baby and I hope we will have the opportunity to spend quality time with him in the future. He is love in its purest light.

I thought it was time to check in again with all of you. Thank you for checking in on the girls and me. Nearly seven weeks ago today, Don's soul ascended and my world fundamentally shifted. Intangible moments rise and bring rivers of tears and sometimes I feel like a leaky pot . . . just little bits spilling out here and there. There's a story about a cracked pot that was being carried but it watered the soil along the way and caused flowers to grow. I don't know if that is what's happening, I just know that there are triggers all around me that can get me leaking. Any act of kindness reminds me of Don. My sister Kathy told me about someone she knew picking up the tab for a bunch of folks and she said, "He did a Don!" My family (Daddy, Kathy, Alene, Jr., and Aunt Lilly) has been my rock and Skye and Liisi bring me joy daily as I see Don in them in so many ways. These things make me smile and weep in the same moment. I sang in Toronto recently and I felt as though I was breathing for Don. I don't know if that makes sense to you but that's how it felt. Music is wonderful therapy for me. I am inspired through my sadness to keep pushing for the things that were important to me and Don; to keep moving forward, upward and onward. I know he would want that for me and the girls. I am striving to be enough of a river people for Don and me. I want my girls to learn the art of giving . . . not just of things, but also of their time and attention to things outside their own needs. It's important to me to reach out to you so we can hold on to each other.

With God's help we are trying to redesign our lives and find a new normal . . . whatever that is. We are heading into choppy waters ahead but your prayers have been our buoys. What I know, is that it is but a breath between life and death. I know that as lonely as I feel, there is gratitude for the 20 years I got to spend with my prince. He left us in such good company with all of you looking out for our wellbeing and caring so deeply about our everyday ordinariness. What I know is that time passes but there is not a moment that passes I don't think of him. And in the seven weeks, God has chosen more beautiful flowers for his heavenly garden. Many of you have shared your losses with me and in many ways, we all grieve together. In our lifetime, we will all experience loss. In Joan Didion's memoir, The Year of Magical Thinking, she says, "Grief turns out to be a place none of us know until we reach it." How true are these words. It doesn't follow a Kubler-Ross method necessarily, of moving through denial, anger, bargaining, and finally acceptance . . . for me it is just these tsunami waves that come at the most unexpected times. Let us keep each other in prayer as we rides the valleys and mountaintops of life; there are many. I am happy that we have a shared faith and a communion with God through prayer. For your love and comfort, I thank you and I ask God's blessings upon all your lives that you may fill your days with Godly deeds, living fully, and here's to hoping you get all your dreams. And as we continue to celebrate Don's legacy, remember to make one of your own. Don would always say, "Make a mark, not a scar."

On our knees,

Wife of Don,

Mother of Skye and Liisi

Chapter 22

TWINKLE, TWINKLE LITTLE STAR

"How I wonder what you are. Up above the world so high, like a diamond in the sky.
Twinkle, twinkle little star."

—Nursery rhyme

Looking back on my journey, I know that in addition to my grieving for myself, I was also grieving for my children: I felt Skye's heartbreak when she first realized, "Dad won't be at my graduation!" I ached for Liisi, who seemed to want to climb into her dad's skin and needed to feel attached to him by keeping clothing or jewelry of his with her at all times.

I watched and wondered how my children were coping with this huge loss of their Dad. Everyone kept asking them, "How are you doing?" They didn't know what to say, they didn't know how they were doing. Surviving was day-to-day, moment-to-moment.

Initially there were lots of tears, but it seems they wanted to be strong for me, feeling that seeing them sad would make me sadder. I told them it's okay to cry and feel sad, but they didn't show much of it in front of me, which caused me greater concern.

I didn't do a lot of crying either, so I tried to let them be. I felt I was carrying everybody: carrying my daughters' worry (though they didn't ask me to), my own worry and sadness, and the spirit of Don in an effort to keep us going. I wanted the girls to give their worries to me, but that would come later. I also learned from some adult friends that they were indeed worried about me.

In the first weeks, the girls wanted to have friends over. The house was much quieter than usual in the evenings when they came home from school. Still, they played their favorite music and talked a lot to each other late at night. I let them; I did not enforce a bedtime because this was their sister time and important bonding time.

On weekends, they had friends their age over, and would not spend so much time together then. I wanted to be sure they stayed bonded to each other in a healthy way for support but they also needed their time with friends. Though they were busy, I tried to have dinner at home most nights when they were not committed to theater group and other outside endeavors. I was feeling my way through this rough period and learned with them as I went.

A few weeks after they were back in school, Liisi's friends gave us a lovely gift. Her eighth-grade class made banners decorated artfully with their inside jokes and sunny messages. We hung them all over the house where she would see them, but they uplifted all of us. We kept going, and it was a busy school year for both on top of our grief.

I didn't want them to feel what I was feeling, but each had her own path in grief and I could not—as much as I wanted to—make it mine. I asked my quieter, introspective Skye, "Did you talk to Daddy today? Did you think about Daddy today?"

And she says, "Yep, I did," with a smile. I wanted to give her permission to continue talking with and about her father.

Chapter 23

HOW DO YOU KEEP
THE MUSIC PLAYING?

"How do you keep the music playing? How do you make it last?
How do you keep the song from fading too fast?"

——James Ingram and Patti Austin

There is no way to plan for the firsts that come after someone you love leaves the physical world. It is no easier to think about moving Don's things out of the house now—three years later—than it was to consider doing it in the very beginning, right after he died.

I remember a couple days after Donnie ascended, Liisi came to my office, sat on my lap, and asked, "What are you going to do with Daddy's clothes? What about his pictures all around the house? They make me sad."

"They'll make you happy in a little while. This is Daddy's house still. This is our home," I told her.

With certainty I knew that everything needed to stay in its place. My children did not need any other changes in their world. Because it had been turned upside down, everything else needed to stay the same. Jeff Hill, our assistant, and Maria Herrera, our dear housekeeper and second mother, were a constant presence in their lives. It helped us so much that they showed up just as before in such a loving way. I wondered how I would help my girls keep the music of their Daddy's life alive. How to keep the song of his beautiful spirit soaring not just for them, but for the voice-over community that called him King? How would I keep the music of our love vibrant?

135

There was much to contemplate as these questions presented themselves on a daily basis. Suddenly everything in our home became more endowed with meaning because Don and I had chosen it: the lived-in walls, the pictures he'd hung there, the furniture, the door handles—I chose to keep our home-life world simple and familiar. I don't know how I knew this to be the right thing to do—call it motherly instinct—but I did. There was no hurry to move anything. I'd heard of some people choosing to move from their homes for various reasons, or packing up their beloved one's belongings in hopes that it would help them move forward. My feelings were just the opposite and in an instant I was certain of it; no consulting was needed on this first of the firsts that the girls and I would walk through without their dad, learning together as we went, holding each other's hands. My decision to leave everything as it was, was validated six weeks after laying my boy to rest when we headed to Pennsylvania. Skye and Liisi were asked to be Christine's maids of honor at her October wedding. It was early fall, with bright colorful trees in abundance in that part of the state. The truth is, it gave us a chance to get out of our routine and environment and breathe the air somewhere else. And I was finally able to read Joan Didion's *The Year of Magical Thinking,* given to me by Steve Susskind's wife.

I read about how Joan couldn't give her husband's shoes away, imagining he was going to walk through the door and need them. I have not given Don's shoes away though we know people who wear his size. I can't part with them because I think, *Who can stand in them?*

So Don's clothes hung in the closet just as they were. His studio, "The Hole," stayed just as it was. It became a sacred space only the children and our closest friends were allowed to enter. Every picture stayed on the walls where it was before Donnie ascended, and that normalcy seemed to fill us with his spirit and love more and more each day. It was one of the things that—looking back—I knew was the best choice for us. By keeping things just as they were, we felt his spirit and presence as they soared and surrounded us like a warm blanket in the cold moments when we missed him so.

Liisi goes to his drawers and chooses some of his boxers to wear to bed and as the winter months come in, she chooses to wear a couple of his oversized sweaters. I wear them too. Skye walks through the closet and touches his jackets. She sees him all around her. They are not ready to part with anything that belonged to their dad; it was their stake in feeling a tiny sense of sameness in the midst of the loss. And as we geared up to face the holidays without Don, only the pictures on the walls and the clothes hanging in the closets provided a sense of anything familiar.

Halloween was Don's favorite holiday. He adored the dress-up aspect, and loved to make it theatrical and artsy. He was a cigar-smoking fairy, complete with tutu and leotards one year, and he built an amazing haunted house in our basement for Liisi another year. He loved helping the girls choose just the right costume; it was so much fun for him.

For our first Halloween without him, we decked the house out in all our accumulated decorations for that season and went trick or treating in one of Liisi's friend's neighborhoods since we didn't get many trick-or-treaters in our neighborhood. Skye went to a small Halloween gathering at one of her friend's, and we met up afterwards and ate at the IHOP since it was empty.

We talked about how much fun Halloween always was for Daddy—how he loved to dress up (we loved getting the candy, though we never ate a sixteenth of it), and how we all loved it, too. I dressed up as Elvira I think, all in good clean fun with my children. I was as willing as their dad had been to do anything to bring a smile to their faces and hear them laugh more often. Still, it was tough for us because this was one of Dad's favorite times of the year. We breathed, did the best we could, and kept going. Don was my Halloween and every-day angel guiding us along this rough path.

We spent that first Thanksgiving together with my family, as had become our tradition for many years—this time in an Arizona resort. For several years, we'd decided this would be our time together as a family, at one of our clan's hometowns or at a nice hotel that served Thanksgiving dinner.

Liisi loved to surf the Web looking for new and fancy hotels and she had come across this one. It was a neutral place and looked great. Best of all, we were all so wound up from our lives' responsibilities, school, and trying to find a new rhythm that massages would be a treat. It was nice to get out of the house and out of town once more. Though we were learning to cope with our loss, coming home to a house without Donnie in it was happy and sad at the same time; happy to be there with all our memories surrounding us but sad that we couldn't hug Daddy.

The next first holiday hurdle coming up was Christmas, our most sacred family time other than family vacation. Since the girls were three and seven years old, we cultivated Christmas mornings as a time at home for memory making, and we'd had some beautiful, love- and squeal-filled early mornings as a family. Coming up to the holidays, I again checked in with my Prayer Village to express what I was learning and what we were feeling.

Tuesday, December 9, 2008, 4:23 PM

Seasons Greeting to all!

Hello prayer village dwellers. I wanted to send you a check-in update last week but I was without internet for several days. So many of you called or invited my family to partake in your Thanksgiving festivities . . . Thank you very much. The girls and I went to a quiet resort in Arizona with my dad and sisters, along with their families, and enjoyed hanging out together along with some much-needed spa treatments for relaxation. The girls even got in on it and had their first facials there, too! Laughing, playing board games, and eating together were just what we needed along with getting out of our environment for a moment. It has been more than 3 months since Don left this earthly place and that feels astounding to me just to say it. As these "first" holidays come, emotions rise and we felt the sting of his loss more acutely. Sometimes the girls will simply say through tears, "I miss Daddy." That of course breaks my heart but these are feelings we are all feeling and giving voice to it somehow lightens it a bit by simply stating it. I remember reading some time ago that when you are going through a challenge, look for the lessons. I've often wondered why a heart has to endure this kind of pain and loss but I believe the lesson for me that I want to share with all of you is pretty obvious. That life is beautiful, fragile and often far too short. We must tell the ones we love how much we love and value them and how much they mean to us. Don't waste a day in anger; you can never get it back and do your very best for those you love.

We are living in a time of loss on many levels compounded by an economy that is fractured and has us all worrying about our world, our planet, and our lives. It is now that we must have a deeper inner dialog and get a hold of something intangible . . . something called faith. If you don't have one, get some! Yes my heart has been broken this year but each of you has had your own share of hard times, hard decisions, and personal challenges as well. Without faith and a belief in a chance to start again, we would just sit in the stew of our "overwhelment" and be paralyzed by our situation. Prayer has been for my family a rock and an anchor in the midst of the storms. Reaching out to you to speak my concerns, to express my emotional place and yearnings has helped me tremendously. Thank you for being there for us; for being in the amazing village of people who have prayed with the girls and me this year especially and help us speak louder to our faith. And as you've helped me, some of that love and prayer has gone right back to you. Dwelling together in the place of faith I feel has somehow strengthened us all. It helps to know that you're not alone; that others are concerned. I think the unhappiest people in the world are those who don't know that someone really cares about them. So in the season of gratitude and gift giving, it is most important to me that I say to all of you that I love you and value your gift of presence in my life and in my girls' lives. Thank you for continuing to hold my hand, for the phone calls and emails of love and concern for me and the girls. I am in a different mindset with Christmas this year. Don and I enjoyed gift giving in a big way, but in this economy, it brings us all back to the real reason for the season; to celebrate and remember the birth of Jesus Christ (yes my Jewish friends Jesus was a Jew so you are included in this too), and that the joy of this season is not just about giving gifts but rather to focus on goodness, joy and gratitude in your own life.

Gift yourself with the power of love and forgiveness. Love brought us all together through the love we collectively share for Don. Spend time with those you love and if you can't do that, find a family or friend to surround yourself with. The end of the year causes us to reflect on all we did, all we wanted to do, and all we want to get done. Finding gratitude where you are right now, even in the midst of crisis and uncertainty, is the biggest gift to yourself. Revel in it! Find laughter! Merry Christmas!

With gratitude and peace,

Nita, Wife of Don, Mother of Skye and Liisi

Preparing for Christmas was heavy. We loved to really decorate for the season but we always needed help because our home is not a usual shape and it's difficult for little ol' me to hang lights. In the past, we hired helpers to assist us with all the decorations and the outside of the house presented its own challenges since it was a contemporary home. We put up the pre-lit tree and were going to add some ornaments later in the trimming phase.

This year, our Christmas decorator, Kleev, asked about using angel wings to adorn the tree with gold ribbons; he was such a lovely, intuitive man and of course the wings were the perfect adornment for the tree and for how this Christmas would feel. A single ten-watt star was placed as the tree topper. Kleev put the lights on a timer so they would come on and go off at a chosen hour.

Around that time I had been talking to Don asking if he could show me a sign from him. A couple people called me to share they'd had an encounter with him, seeing him on television or in a dream, but I had not.

"Show me something, Donnie, to let me feel you . . . See you," I begged.

About five days before Christmas, I was awakened in the middle of the night by Jack, my six-pound toy poodle and the oldest of our four dogs, yelping persistently to be let out of his kennel. This didn't happen often. My door was closed and when I opened it to head downstairs to the kitchen and let him out I noticed a bright light filling the two-story space of my sitting room. I was so sleep-muddled that I wondered aloud why that starlight had not gone out. I went down and tried to figure out where the outlet was so I could unplug it, but I didn't find it and Jack's barks were growing louder.

I let him out and waited in the kitchen for him to return from doing his business. I sat with my eyes closed. After he was petted and placed back in his kennel, I walked through the sitting room again, with that warm light filling the space, and decided I would figure it out tomorrow.

The next day, I talked with our friend and asked him about the star and the timer. It was then that he informed me all the lights were on one timer and it should have gone off with the rest of the lights at eleven o'clock. So that was my sign, and I was too sleepy to get it when it was happening. I do remember not only seeing the warm light but feeling it, too. That was my Don. That moment was not only Divine it was Don-Vine!

When we get to Christmas my children said the sweetest things about their dad: "Mom, we get it, Dad *was* Santa! With his little cherub cheeks, and always giving and helping . . . he was the Dude!"

Their comment warmed my heart because so much of his giving was quiet, but they did see it. Still, the deep-seated sadness and anxiety of how I would handle this first Christmas alone weighed heavily upon me.

One of my lovely neighbors, Jillian, gave me some sage words of advice that I would call upon during difficult times: "Don't anticipate it, just let it be."

Some advice given in a pamphlet called "When Your Spouse Dies" suggested we create some new rituals along with the old. We had started a small surprise hunt but I decided I would add this in as our new ritual actually started by Kleev leaving some goodies hidden for the girls. I was up late creating clues that rhymed and placing the surprises to make it really special. But on Christmas morning as we headed downstairs to the tree, we remembered that Donnie always got the video camera.

Liisi looked at me and simply asked, "Are you going to get the camera, Mom?"

"Yes," I simply said.

I didn't know if we would spend the whole day crying, or really what to expect. I had invited a couple of close friends who always made the children laugh to share the day with us and to my surprise, one of them arrived in a full Santa suit with fresh doughnuts, and we laughed the morning away. Later that evening we had dinner with my friends the Dworskys. I hadn't expected much joy that day except to see my girls opening their gifts and trying hard not to let missing Daddy consume our day. I am reminded that angels don't have to be invisible or mystical always; they can walk among us. It was a beautiful day.

The New Year came quickly on a warm, bright winter morning as I went outside to do some morning chores. It was warm enough to go barefoot, and I loved feeling the sun wash over me, as did this year's beginning. I began to sweep the limestone outside the back doors of our home, which I've done since I was a little girl. I was alone with my thoughts as the birds sang to me in the morning glow. While sweeping I had an epiphany, which I shared with my daughters. Then I reached out to the Prayer Village, family, and friends to share what had occurred to me while sweeping. My girls told me I was weird.

Sweeping   01/02/10

Today I swept. It's a bright January day after the New Year has turned and the quiet beginning of a new decade in a sunny sixty-eight degrees. It started when I was doing poop duty; picking up the droppings here and there of our four dogs (not my favorite thing to do, yet necessary) and that led to the beginning of sweeping. There was so much dirt that was covering the off-white limestone of the back landing that I didn't really know it was there until I started sweeping. When I started, it didn't look dirty at all, just a bit dingy in places but as I swept I noticed that there was a fine layer covering almost every surface of the limestone. The more I swept I thought about the gardeners who would come and blow it to simply move it, only to land someplace else on my property. A good wind could come and redistribute it again. And how mopping it would make the not so visible dirt wet and soggy and though it gets some of it up, it presses the dirt wetly into the fine crevices of the limestone already made of sand so that still some dirt remains. There were the corners that when looked at closer upon examination had collected the most dirt and was the most obvious. This required extra work on my part to remove it because it seemed to be very happy to be in that shaded place. Something about sweeping and seeing how much dirt is there when we really don't know it and moving it into small piles to be scooped and discarded caused me to see that this sweeping is a metaphor for life.

I know that as we go about our days, life happens; the tragedies, triumphs, sorrows and joys, the good and the bad. Some of it leaves a residue on our spirit much like the dirt on the limestone that is not easily seen. We can move around in it feeling low, depressed and not really understanding why or how we cannot lift this dark, depressed feeling; why this "heaviness" just won't go away. I am learning that it takes a defining moment to help us look at this covering left by a big life storm like sickness, death, debt, divorce, or just being tired of being sick and tired, not getting what we've worked for, to cause us to the get the broom of life out and begin to find our lively God filled spirit that has been slowly covered by the winds that change our lives and leave its residue. Then the corners . . . they require extra attention and extra work to get them cleaned out . . . These are the places that we are so comfortable in; whether it's a broken relationship, repeating unhealthy patterns, staying in victim mode, enabling our children or having children that behave badly or make wrong choices, self-defeating attitudes; this is where our excuses for not rising to the best of ourselves lays. If we really want to sweep away the layers of dust that cloud our lives, we must begin with the corners. This takes inner work, prayer, and really looking at your own stuff and owning it. There is nothing stopping you from co-creating with God the most abundant life possible, except you! As I say this to you I say it to myself. I have the gift of free will. The gardeners of our lives that tell us to just forget about it, it will go away, it will get better, it will blow over, will come, but until we begin to sweep, scoop and really deal with those things that hold us in a place of darkness, we are not truly free. Choose life.

My sweet husband Don ascended and it felt as though an earth-shaking volcano had erupted and spewed a mountain of ash over my life. I had no idea if I would ever see the sun again and many days I wondered if I could truly smile again after crying myself to sleep for months. I had no idea where the shovel was (this was too much for a broom), that I needed to dig myself out and head toward the light of life so I could lead my children to it also. I knew I had to but I didn't know how. The miracle for me was that my family and friends showed up with their shovels of love, prayer, and concern and began to dig toward me heaping away the ash and you kept reaching for me and I reached for you. Your love pulled me toward the light at the end of the tunnel and Don was pushing from the other side. Thank you so much. Though I realize not all the ash is gone, at least I am not under the mountain I once felt. There is still some dust that remains as I move toward healing that time holds, but I know with God's love and grace and with the way you all have covered us with hugs, love and compassion, I am on my way. Perhaps with such a loss, all of the ash and dirt will never be completely gone but I sweep a little every day. As it gets clearer for me, I hope it does for my girls too. I have to be their beacon now. The more I swept today, the clearer it became to me that life is a sweeping journey and whether you have cobwebs, skeletons, a mountain of ash or just a fine layer, it requires your attention to details to continue to clean it out. Love is in the details and God is the love. Don't be afraid of the light, or a clearer view. It's a new year for a clearer you. Sweep it. Scoop it, let it go. Choose love.

Valentine's Day arrived. I had a granite grave marker made engraved with Don's name, date of birth, the dash, and the day he left the world. The dash was where his life was lived but how can one sum up a life in a dash? As I placed that marker at his gravesite I absorbed the words I chose for the inscription: "The Voice of Our Hearts."

With my heart still breaking, I knew God gives us the will and power to survive these moments of tremendous sadness. Light does come in through this darkness, from calls of concern, talks and walks with loving friends, laughter, making music, and mostly from my children. Don would always buy me something lovely: a bauble, something romantic, and always dinner out. My thought in a moment of self-pity and loneliness was, "He thought me wonderful. Who will ever see me that way again? Who will ever love me like that?" It was delightful to have someone love me like Don did. The music of love keeps playing through the memories we made together. Our love was a beautiful song we loved to sing. I would always look at him and marvel at how much more in love with each other we were now than on the day we got married, after the years and the memories and building a life together.

We didn't know it was possible our love could grow like that. But if love is deeply rooted in friendship, it gets deeper. And then you have children. And you survive going through a rough time. Love deepens. And then comes the loss. The physical—the hugs and kisses, the embraces, the bumping into him at night in our bed—isn't just for tactile sensations, yet the depth of the love remains. I tell the girls I'm still so in love with Dad and all that he was. All he showed us and how much he loved and adored us. The essence of who he was—the class, silliness, and largesse of him as well as the small obedient boy from Duluth—made so much good out of his life.

Chapter 21

LOVE WILL BUILD A BRIDGE

*"I would whisper love so loudly every heart could understand /
that love and only love can join the tribes of man. / I would give my heart's desire /
so that you might see the first step is to realize that it all begins with you and me."*

—The Judds

Sitting on my white leather recliner surrounded by dogs big and small running amuck, I am listening to my daughters giggling for the last two hours at various silliness, miming, and watching YouTube videos—just the two of them. Their sounds suddenly fill me with a powerful joy, the kind of joy that is peaceful, quiet, and deep. They are giggling. We are together, though one less, as a family having survived many firsts. This feeling is a first too as some light begins to glimmer from the darkness we have felt. It is in this moment I know we are going to make it. Our family love had built a bridge that would carry us over and through the highs and lows of our individual and collective journeys through grief. In our home, we are able to feel at peace, because my beloved is always here.

This home is filled with the essence of my husband. His spirit fills the open spaces and his loving hands touched every door handle, chair, towel rack, and custom toilet paper holder. He is the husband who decided with me that we would build this place and imbue it with the light of family love. This home—whose every room was blessed by our trusted, beloved Pastor Larry, is again ringing with laughter.

Just a couple of nights ago, Liisi quietly walked into my office after midnight where I was fiddling on the computer. She sat in my lap and said, "I miss Daddy."

It is at these moments that I feel most inept and impotent. The nurse and occasional shrink inside me want to fix it. I want to make her sadness go away. It is what I do. But nothing comes to me. I hugged her and simply said, "So do I honey."

We embraced and her tears flowed, washing through me like a roaring river. I didn't fall apart, but I wanted to; I wanted to carry the sadness I was absorbing from her in this moment.

I talked her into coming to lie in my bed (where they always go when they don't feel good, have a bad dream, or feel scared) and prayed for the right words.

The sadness slithered out like a thick black snake and moved down the hallway, penetrating every door, wall, and hardwood floor panel down to the carpet in the TV room and up over the overstuffed sofa into the next blue carpeted guest room with its coordinated bedspread, roman shades, and green and orange accent pillows. It continued on, moving like a dark, smoky plague over the house, then it hung like a thick gray cloud full of heavy tears over every orifice of the custom cinder brink pillars, walls, and even the white baby grand covered with photos of our life and family.

"I'm overwhelmed, Mom. I've got acne that won't go away, too much homework that I wait till the last minute to do. I miss Daddy. No one else that dances has boobs my size. I miss Daddy. I'm scared. Haiti? What's going on? I miss Daddy."

I just held her and told her I was there. I silently prayed. I told her over and over, "I'm here! You're gonna be okay. I won't let you fall."

I wondered what my Skye was feeling that she was not expressing to me. I was hugging her in my heart as I held Liisi, praying she was getting it out, not holding it in.

I expected to feel sad as we began our journey through grief, but I didn't expect to feel scared; scared that I would not know enough to carry them, not have the right words to ease their troubled hearts, or help them know they could feel safe with just me.

I heard Liisi's adolescent angst and hormones, but I also heard her grief. My words felt empty because though I have a beautiful and deep faith and relationship with God, I couldn't promise her nothing bad would happen again or that someone else she loves wouldn't die. I know I couldn't promise her anything beyond this moment. I prayed for strength and courage.

Sleep finally came to her and me, but I woke at five thirty that morning to be sure Skye was getting ready for her school day. The weeping one slept in, too emotionally wrecked to pull on a poker face for school and classmates. The lioness in me told me to keep her going, but I relented that day.

She awoke with slightly swollen eyes, pulled on a pair of Daddy's way-too-big sweats and one of his sweatshirts, and headed down to eat—a good sign on this chilly, rainy day. Slowly the sadness retreated like the low tide of the ocean revealing hidden beauty once again.

I realize now, on this giggling day that it is a mountain moment compared to the pit of black fog two nights ago, when the sadness hovered over my home like a soggy wet blanket.

It is like that, this thing called grief. It feels like raging waters and calm seas. It comes in waves—sometimes tsunamis—that do retreat. Then joy sings for a while.

Sometimes it's me who is the weeping one, though it tends to happen with strangers . . . I don't really know why. I am sure my daughters feel it, in their own way. I remember a time or long for his physical touch, or see a framed picture—there are so many unknown triggers that can become small heart mines that explode with the sad reality of death and its slow, smoldering aftermath. But today—right now—is good and happy, and my girls are home together and an invisible band of love shared by our collective heartbeats connects us. It is an Oh-So-Happy Day, and I'll take it!

I remembered the feeling when we were all in the house together, the girls up in their rooms, Don in his studio. It's a feeling that I cherished because I knew even then that the love in our home was very special. I had known it in my home growing up. There was a feeling of wholeness and wellbeing with us all and we had cultivated a home that was peaceful, loving, and open. It is still peaceful and open in our home.

I began to feel grateful, even in this year of tough firsts, for all that I have, all that I've been blessed with. I began to feel gratitude for my life; that I was still here and able to carry our girls forward. Grateful for all the people—the Village as, it were—that made camp around us, stood in the gap for us, prayed for and over us; the rock that my family is and continues to be, and the friends. Gratitude came fully to me as I slowly awakened from the grip of grief and loneliness. This home, built by our voices, has always been full of life. Our lives were brought together by our voices, and our love helped me keep going. I began to feel a sliver of that life force seeping back into me.

In the quiet moments in my bedroom, I say good morning and goodnight to Don as I say my morning and evening prayers. I feel his presence in this home, and I am getting to know myself in a new way. I am fortified in this home that has always been a source of joy and life. The love that I feel for Don and for the life he worked to give us has been a bridge to so much love, laughter, and grand memories with our family and friends. Don and I quietly believed that if we could bridge the love in our home out to the world, it would be a happier more peaceful place.

Chapter 25

BUTTERFLY KISSES

*"All the precious time like the wind, the years go by. Precious butterfly—
spread your wings and fly. / Oh, with all that I've done wrong I must have done
something right. / To deserve your love every morning / and butterfly kisses at night."*

—Bob Carlisle

There are so many signs that Don sends me to let me know he is happy and that
he is okay. Even before the "starlight" night the previous Christmas I became more
aware of his angelic presence. A couple of months after Donnie passed, I noticed
orange butterflies showing up a lot more than ever before. Initially, I didn't think
much of it, but as I saw them more and more, I believed he was trying to tell me
something.

Often when I'd walk outside or while sitting at a red light, an orange butterfly
would flutter by. This was happening almost daily. Once I was sitting out in the grass
playing with my dogs and one beautiful, large-winged butterfly circled around my
head three times and landed right near my fingertips. I sat very still, wanting it to
stay.

Skye began to see them too, and felt the same connection to them that I did.
Somehow, just when I needed to be reminded that Don's love was still around us,
we'd get an orange butterfly. After nose kisses, ear, forehead, and chin kisses for the
girls at night, we'd always end with the butterfly kisses, which always elicited giggles
from the giver and receiver: a flutter touch that caused a warm, loving sensation.
As I began to recognize these beautiful, orange kisses from Don, I would giggle and
feel a small flutter of excitement and joy. His spirit is still abundantly with us and
making us laugh . . . still.

Our dear friend Pastor Larry Keene continued to minister to me and soothe me with his wise words and sincere love for Don and our family. He captured Don's essence in these words:

> "If a person is able to make the world laugh ONCE, he or she will invariable try to make it laugh again for a SECOND time. And, if the world will laugh again for that second time he or she will be providentially destined to a lifetime of humorous social interaction with their surrounding world. And when that person passes from this stage to another, we who were the willing audience of such artful givings will be left with the echoes of life lifting laughter that will brighten our depressing rainy days and will continue to mend those fractured places in our broken hearts. Be blessed with his memory."

I still see them, the orange butterflies, from time to time, and they seem to show up just when I need to be reminded that like the butterfly, the girls and I have been through a transformative experience. Then I discovered an article by Ina Woolcott that explained in great detail what butterflies symbolize to Native Americans. Her description is profound and confirms my conviction that Donnie was showing himself to us through these gorgeous winged creatures.

> Native Americans see the butterfly as a symbol of joy. Feeding on the flowers they help pollinate, they further spread beauty. Butterflies eyes consist of thousands of individual lenses. This gives them the gift of being able to see a single image clearly. They can perceive ultraviolet wavelengths of light, suggesting clairvoyant abilities for those with Butterfly as power animal. The antennae of the butterfly has small knobs on each end which are said to aid orientation. If an antennae is missing the butterfly will fly in circles unable to find its way. If butterfly is your ally you need to remain consciously connected to spirit at all times so you may fulfill your goals.
>
> Butterfly is the symbol of change, the soul, creativity, freedom, joy and colour. Their power is transformation, shape shifting and soul evolution. They represent the element of air, quickly changing and always on the move gracefully. Butterflies are messengers of the moment and come in a wide array of colours. Studying these colours can help you uncover butterflies message to you. It reminds us not to take things too seriously and to get up and move. They teach us that growth and transformation does

not have to be a traumatic experience. It can be joyous. Butterflies possess the ability to grow and change, leaving the safety of their cocoon to discover a new world in a new form without fear, trusting their untested wings to fly without a doubt in their minds. They work through many important stages to become the beautiful creature they are. Similar to the butterfly, we too are always moving through different stages, each equally as vital. It is no good rushing to a particular stage, nor is it good getting stuck at a stage and becoming stagnant. Butterfly is a potent symbol for those considering, or in the throes of, a big change. Butterfly is also one of the most inspiring symbols of the animal world, knowing precisely the time to leave the comfort and limitation of its cocoon, flying freely into the world. Quite frequently, we are not so certain. The cocoon of our thoughts and fears may be limiting, they are also safe and familiar. We can become afraid of what may be outside of our limiting thoughts and belief systems, trapping us and holding us back from ourselves, from our dreams and desires, from our unlimited potential . . .

Butterfly can help you see that exiting the cocoon suddenly opens a new door, that there is power in trust and vulnerability. No more than you does a butterfly know whether it can fly, but it opens its wings in perfect confidence, and discovers that their delicacy allow its graceful flight, its dance in the air. When we understand that transformation can be as natural as breathing, when we take ourselves lightly, when we trust in our own untried wings to support us, we learn the message of Butterfly, life itself is a joyous dance. Dance brings us the sweetness of life.

Chapter 26

I'LL BE SEEING YOU

"I'll be seeing you in every lovely summer's day and everything that's bright and gay
I'll always think of you that way. I'll find you in the morning sun and when
the night is new; I'll be looking at the moon but I'll be seeing you."

—Tony Bennett

One night around March, I found myself surfing the internet, crying, trying to
find some unturned stone that I may have missed in Don's treatments, something
I should have known about. Skye was away at school and Liisi walked in and sat on
my lap, seeing me cry. Her fourteen-year-old wisdom spoke to me and said, "Daddy
doesn't want us to be sad, Mommy. He wants us to be happy."

Here was my child comforting me, and it somehow seemed strange and perfect
at the same time. The nights were always the hardest for me. It was the time Don
and I would spend together after his day of recording sessions and mine of running
around taking care of everything else as well as the occasional auditions. We'd talk in
our tub built for two and make plans for our lives. Whether we were checking in on
the girls or shepherding homework, the evenings were a time for togetherness, and
now they were when I missed Don most.

In the *Art of Resilience,* author Carol Orsborn wrote about taking an "emotional
vacation." The girls and I had been going at a very busy pace, getting through the
holidays and Valentine's Day, sending out college and high school applications,
waiting for results, getting through the school year and extracurricular activities . . .
We had not stopped to feel fully what our minds, spirits, and bodies had undergone.

I remembered how much the girls loved Hawaii and how safe they felt there. I
decided at that moment this was exactly what we needed as a family. We needed a

dose of Hawaii to soothe our emotional states of being and to be together without the distraction of our daily lives. I planned it all without their knowledge or consent.

I packed their bags and surprised them the day we were going to the airport. Skye was told she was being picked up for an orthodontic appointment. Liisi woke up to me holding a fake lei saying, "Surprise, Liisi! We're going to Hawaii. I love you!"

She thought I had lost my mind.

Skye was stunned and thrilled as she walked to the car realizing that she wasn't going for an orthodontic adjustment after all. Neither of them could believe it, but were as thrilled about going as I was to take them to a place of respite that held such beautiful memories for our family. It was just what the doctor ordered, and an investment of quality time with my girls.

We zip-lined, got henna tattoos, played at the beach, and watched the sun set. Lovely. We had such an awesome bonding time, and the ocean sounds felt as though they washed away some of our deep-seated sadness. It was very healing. Sitting at the ocean's edge watching one sunset, we saw three whales frolicking in the distance. It reminded me of the three of us, learning to play again. Seeing the vastness and the grand scale of the ocean helps to put one's life in perspective.

One day at the ocean, I noticed a painter standing on the sand painting a seascape. We stopped to observe his process. An introduction followed and he asked our names. When I said Liisi's name, he replied that he had swam with a dolphin named Liisi. He looked over at us with kind blue eyes and salt-and-pepper curls gently peeking from under his sun hat. We talked more about some paintings he had displayed, and I asked if he finger-painted or taught at a Waldorf school. Our children had attended a Waldorf school in their early years and I recognized the technique in one of the paintings on display nearby.

In spite of the day's grey April weather, he started his current painting by covering the canvas in bright yellow paint as if to invoke the sun within the painting. As we talked, I learned that his last name was Freeheart. I felt that it fit him, seeing his kind eyes.

Suddenly he paused and said, "I feel a need to add an angel to this picture."

I had said nothing of our loss, or that this was our first trip without Don. The girls and I looked at each other and Skye said softly to me, "Mom, that's Dad."

I knew she was right.

Mr. Freeheart sketched an angel with open arms in the upper left of the painting, the rest of it to be filled in later. We went on with our day, knowing that again Don was sending us loving reminders that he was with us.

I had taken Mr. Freeheart's business card and tried to connect with him a day or so later to see if he had finished the painting, but we missed each other. After the girls and I returned home, I sent him an email reminding him who we were and inquired about the painting. He told me he had named it *Angel on the Beach* and attached a copy of it in the email.

It took my breath away. The angel was painted into the seascape as a large white cloud with arms wide open and inviting, looming large and gentle and welcoming above the painted blue ocean and sloping mountains. Only then did I share our loss with the artist, and how we felt he had been a conduit that day on the beach.

I have that painting in my home today. Without a doubt, I know Don sent us a message that day and he is watching over us.

When we returned home, rested and relaxed, I found myself reflecting on many thoughts and ideas that the trip had inspired.

Where does peace live? Is it a place or a state of being? The ups and downs, twists and turns of one's journey are so puzzling to me still. There is no way to know the road, to measure joy or sadness, to expect the unexpected or to know how you will feel when you meet your baby for the first time. Will you mate for life or have several marriages or dalliances? If you're a good parent, will your children be normal or above average? What will your life's work be and will it change or grow? Why do disasters happen and how do people that survive them survive? How do you live after the love of your life dies? How can you be Mom and Dad for them? Do we know when it is our time to die?

There are so many questions about unknown, anxiety-inducing experiences you can only understand once you are in them. In that lies the peace that comes hand-in-hand for me with faith. Faith is the foundation my soul's journey is built on and its grace carries me through. Though questions remain and experiences teach and heartbreak happens and joy rises, it is the treasure of each day that keeps us moving forward. That is why it is called it life; the unpredictabilities, the mountaintops and valley lows—the moments that give you breath or take it away, are all a part of its road.

Chapter 27

THE GREATEST LOVE OF ALL

"Let the children's laughter remind us how we used to be."

—Whitney Houston

I appreciate now more than ever that Christine, Skye, and Liisi had a father like Don, so involved in every aspect of their lives, and that I had a husband like him. He wanted the best for us and gave us the best of himself. From this place of gratitude tinged with pain and longing I grew to see that the light was never dulled because of the love I've known. Don gave us a great big, beautiful, unconditional love, and that love keeps the light bright as a beacon guiding me as we navigate this new part of my life.

The first anniversary of Don's death was a sunny day, not unlike the startlingly bright day he ascended. I decided we needed to be together as a family. Even though it was a weekday, Liisi and I flew to northern California to be with Skye, who was settling into her new life as a freshman college student. Her first day of classes began on September 1; I knew this could not be an easy day for her. I wanted us to be together on this day. Whatever they would feel, we would have each other to lean on.

Landing at around nine thirty, we picked up a rental car, some food for the dorm, and some white flowers at Costco. I knew I wanted to do something special to commemorate the day, but beyond flying up there, I didn't have a clue what that would be. I prayed and asked for guidance. My chest was tight from anticipation.

Skye looked small and tender as we watched her come back to her dorm from her first class. I couldn't wait to hug her. She was excited and scared being there in her new life away from the security of home.

I felt us trying so hard to keep it together. Each of us was afraid that if one broke down, we'd all start to wail.

We talked about Daddy and what he would say about her going off to college, how he would poke fun at this or that, and how he was proud of where she was, but we did not talk about his death or his services or any of the hard stuff. If one of us had opened that up, it could have broken us and stopped the day. Instead we focused on the living wonderful reflections of him that made us smile and laugh; it was easy enough to cry, which we all did in our separate beds. I wanted us to never stop talking about him in that beautiful way.

We went through the drive-in at In and Out Burger in honor of Don, who loved them so.

I found a lake not far from the school and decided we would go there. We took the white flowers that I'd purchased, walked to a wooden platform close to the lake's edge with the aggressive ducks crowding around us hoping for food, and I had the Divine insight to ask the girls to speak thanks for what their Dad had meant to them. There were only two flights daily to her school, and we had to be on the six forty flight the same day, so we had to make every moment count.

I began by thanking Donnie for loving me so beautifully and for filling my heart. Our hearts were full and we were on the edge of tears yet we were smiling.

Next, Liisi said, "Thanks, Dad, for showing me what class looks like."

And Skye said, "Thanks, Dad, for raising the bar so high."

I was bursting with pride at how they "got" their Dad and knew what a great man he was . . . and how much he loved them.

We tossed the white flowers into the water along with a little of our worries and sadness. Skye later said it was a turning point for our family; she was becoming more insightful and wise.

While we were on the way to drop Skye at her dorm, Christine called from Florida, full of emotion. United, we acknowledged our love for him. We said our goodbyes, dropped Skye back at her dorm, then Liisi and I headed to the airport.

Since that first anniversary I keep accepting grief and touching the hand of grace on my journey now. So clear are these grace-filled moments that now, when I reflect on how I learned to embrace the sadness of our grief and not ignore it, I can see how Don helped teach us—especially me—what living really is; to expect the unexpected and to dance with life. All the ways he lived so large, loved so fully, gave so freely, and filled his corner of the sky with kindness would be lessons in grace from the earth-angel boy who hid his wings. One of the many gifts he gave to me was starting me on the road to receiving grace long before I understood grief and other challenges could be its companion. My heart is open so I can see what is being shown to me.

Chapter 28

TWENTY-ONE-MONTH-OLD BABY

There are days that I feel like a toddler, running about and figuring out so many different things in my new world. A little more than twenty-one months ago my husband Don passed away, yet I still ask, *How can this be? He was just here.*

As I pass a photograph with his smiling eyes looking back at me, it still seems unbelievable and new, and at other times it feels like it's been ten years since I've seen his face.

Even though I have the grand and precious responsibilities of continuing to raise our teenage daughters, there are days that I want to sit in the crib of my life and have things brought to me, have someone pick me up, calm my fears, help dry my tears, and tell me it's okay. But we must keep moving forward remembering to breathe.

Those first weeks after the assault of his ascension and the twister wreckage I found myself inside, it felt like my bag of waters had burst and I was coming, willing or not, into a new place. I was being moved out of the safe comfort of the womb that Don and I had created and into a new world. There were hands all over me helping me to breathe, patting my back, wiping me down, and wrapping me tightly in blankets of love. I was a quivering blob of flesh completely dependent on others to move me from one thing to the other in those first days. My eyes began to open, and I was able to focus on things in this new altered universe, yet wanting so badly to go back to my womb where I knew I was safe. And so I began with the simplest things, eating (sometimes), sleeping (not too much), pooping, and repeat. For a baby this age, not gaining weight is called Failure to Thrive. I was failing. I called it the Losing Your Husband Diet. Surely there was a gentler way to get slim. The world seemed and felt so different then.

The next three to six months I learned to crawl a little. It was more or less a scootch. As family had to leave, I was there to get my daughters through their school year, one with applications into college, the other into a new high school, and to remain their constant. I was subject to sudden fits of crying in the most unusual places. I was worried about them and they were worried about me. I was learning to support my own weight like babies this age do while holding onto a hand. God was holding mine. I was testing out my legs in preparation for eventual walking. For babies this is the time also of hand and foot discovery and certainly I spent time lying on my back rediscovering who I was and how it was all working and how I was going to navigate this new universe.

Then comes the stranger anxiety of the six- to nine-month-old baby that I was, but instead, I experienced friend anxiety. I didn't want anyone I knew to ask me how I was doing. My answer was always, "I don't know, I've never been here before. But I'm standing."

I avoided being in places where people could ask me that question. They were so willing to help but often didn't know how, and I didn't know how to let them. But gradually I began to feel more social. I started to make my own sounds and form some new words. Everything goes in the mouth at this age and I began to eat again and fill out. (Yes, baby got her back, back!) Still the world looked different, and every day I was discovering new things about my world and about myself. That I could sit without falling over; that was new, too.

After one year, I learned to walk and though I wasn't sure-footed or steady and sometimes I still fell, I was in forward motion. Much of the months before this were spent in the same places since I had not really learned my mobility. During this time, my daughter was headed to college and I, with my newfound mobility, had to be sure she got there and had everything that she needed.

Again there were many hands helping me, sending wonderful gifts of support and love for her moving to this new part of her life. She, too, I am sure, felt many of the same things that I was feeling. We got through it without much separation anxiety because she came home whenever she needed, and I needed that, too. Healing has no timetable. My younger daughter was stronger than I ever imagined and we continued to talk daily about Daddy and all the fun we had.

And so we continued to grow and the world got a little brighter once we got some distance from the traumatic rebirth that death causes. At fifteen months, I was a chatterbox. My words began coming in and I still didn't feel like my whole self because I was halved by his departure. But my legs were working better now and I was on the move. Still I cried, but still I rose. The girls held me up and I held them up. We prayed together a prayer of gratitude every night for the love we've known and the love we've been shown. We were grateful for our faith and that our hearts tethered us to something greater than the pain of grief we felt. I saw orange butterflies in abundance at the most unusual places and I was reminded there is still wonder in the world; wonder that God still gives us to see and to let us know that our angels are sending us gentle whispers. I talked to them all the time.

It's twenty-one months now, and I am almost out of my Pull-Ups and trying on my big-girl panties. It, too, feels different, but I am trying to embrace it for what it is. I am relearning to embrace life for what it is: a gift. Though the sadness ebbs and flows with an unpredictability of a twenty-one-month-old baby's outburst, life is still an adventure that we are left here to explore. I, along with my girls, my family, my friends and my faith climb aboard a new boat headed for uncharted waters and new horizons. As Elizabeth Lesser says:

> *I am learning to hold health and sickness, weakness and strength, and even life and death side by side-two sides of one coin. I am learning that it is never either-or, but both and more. Not life or death but life and death, health and sickness, good and bad. Both and something more. I am learning to love the human condition, to say a full and rousing yes to it all, to work with it, to choose it, just as it is, every day.*

I, with my toddler spirit, my twenty-one-month-old self, and ever-focusing eyes couldn't agree more.

Chapter 29

LOVELY DAY

Then I look at you and the world, alright with me.

Then I know it's going to be——a lovely day.

———

—Bill Withers

Trying to quiet my mind is not often easy. It tends to rush forward to the next thing that needs to get done. I keep telling my mind to go to a vacant beach, or to focus on a dark starlit sky, yet the crows chattering out *Caw! Caw!* in the distance, the low hum of the lawn mower down the street, and the rumble of car and truck engines passing nearby keep pulling me back.

What a glorious lovely day today! The sun has broken through and shines up the green hillsides and grassy areas of Los Feliz, after our much-needed recent rains. There is more color here than I've seen in two years. My heart feels open and light. These days I find myself moving about my life in this new husbandless normal with a bit more ease. Sometimes I feel guilty about that—that I should be somehow sadder for the world to see. I know that's crazy, but I remember once reading a card (at a car wash, of all places) whose words come back to me now: Don't wear your sorrow as a sign of how much you loved another, but wear joy as a testament to that love.

Nearly three years after losing Don, I am still finding my voice in a world without his. We now have two grandsons and the youngest has a mouth just like his grandfather; I wonder if he will have the voice. I am blessed to live in a home we love. Our girls are thriving, creating, and growing. Writing this and sharing our story of love is helping me and healing me. I offer this to all of you as my testimony that love survives and faith is necessary to ground you through the storm of loss.

Recently I heard a life motto from a young philosopher named Matthew Stepanek who died at age thirteen but was wise beyond his years. He said, "We must play after every storm."

That resonated fully with me because I believe I am learning to do just that and it is something I hope we all learn to do. I wish the pain of grief for no one but we know that death is still a part of life; we should speak more freely about it before we get to those sad, unfathomable moments. The meaning of the word "suffer" is to "feel keenly," so the lows of the depth of loss can be followed by great joy because we feel it all.

I live in a consciousness of gratitude and a spirit of peace. I am learning that at those moments you think your life is done because the pain is so great, just hold on and hang in there. It gets better . . . it gets lighter.

Mark Nepo's *Book of Awakening* teaches that you can have the life you want by being present to the life you have. Love is on the way and there truly is a blessing after the storm if you open your heart to living. I learned so much from living with a man who loved his life and his family that way; he enjoyed every morsel of being alive.

America's favorite girlfriend, Oprah, once said she believed that "death is a wakeup call to live more fully." This is indeed true. My world is colored with more love than I could have imagined at this point. My voice is here on these pages, though singing is still what I love. For twenty-two years, I sang in harmony with one of the greatest voices of our generation. It was a perfect harmony but through grace and mercy I am learning it is okay to sing solo once more. Don, for all you taught me, and how you loved me, I thank you. And for everyone whose life intersected with yours, I am sure they want to thank you, too. It's a different world without you and your voice in it, but your voice, your spirit, your courage, and your heart will stand as a model for us all.

Talking with a person living with cancer, I asked him what he had learned. He in turn asked me what I had learned living through the illness and loss of my beloved. I had to think for a moment but what I know now is that this experience has brought gratitude into a clearer and higher meaning in my life.

I always felt that I had a big attitude of gratitude, but everything suddenly meant more since the moment we learned of Don's health challenge. Every gesture, look, and hug held more significance. Each day that I could roll over and see those amazing blue eyes looking at me and to hear that baritone saying "Good morning, honey" was like a breath of fresh air (minus the morning breath, that is).

Laughter was heightened, our Scrabble games held more quality, and meals together as a family were as meaningful as a Thanksgiving feast. I felt I could not do enough, give enough, or be near him enough. It wasn't fanatical. I was so honored to give him the highest care and love that I could bring forth. Does that make sense? I've always been the kind of wife who enjoyed doing special things for my husband and my family, though we gave each other space to be free and grow personally and in our careers. But I have learned gratitude in a different way. Looking at the sky or a butterfly has a renewed sense of wonder and gratitude for the beauty that it gives me. That's grace.

Love doesn't end when a loved one dies, it evolves into something deeper, purer, higher, more beautiful and sacred. There is a comforting presence that I am aware of at all times. Remembering the way he'd love to surprise us on our trips with golden boxes in our hotel room or on cruise ship beds with some trinket he'd found for us as a keepsake. When we'd see them, he would give a cherub-cheeked half-smile/half-grin, eyebrows raised, eyes twinkling. We always felt extremely blessed in the life we were allowed. We took none of our favor for granted particularly because Don had a great desire to give back because he'd been given so much. That's Don.

What joys our hearts knew I could never try to fully capture in words; it was a heart-expanding experience with soul. In a word, splendid. Grace shows its face in mundane kindness and love's embraces just when we need it. What remains is a growing peace in the gratitude I feel for having walked for twenty-two years with my soul-mate and best friend. The sadness is there but it gets quieter and doesn't scream quite as loud.

There are women and men who are on this road that takes us through grief to a place of mourning on the way to healing. Some are farther along and others are behind me but we all share the same intimate loss; the love of our lives. Several of you reading this have walked this road before me. I know that I have to carry my girls into their lives and that is my charge. My intention is to be the best I can be for them and still try to remember to take care of myself (haven't gotten so good at that one yet). To remember that I need to continue to sing because that is how I can start to heal my broken heart. Music and prayer have that power for me. Thank you for letting me share my journey with you.

We've been able to find laughter in the darkness, sunshine in the rain, and hope even in despair. I am growing and learning to trust God even more and know that He really has my back. My daughters' faces, laughter, and love fill some of the broken places in my cracked heart, but there is always an empty space for Don that is only filled by reliving the many wonderful moments that we shared. And these moments that I get to share with you bring me farther on my road to healing. The road through grief to grace is a long one, but I am equipped with the garment of God's love, the shoes of hope springs eternal, the crown of family favor and blessings, and the song of Don's love in my heart.

Revel in the moments.

Epilogue

There is a folk story that tells of a family who lived in a village and was robbed while they were away. In their great room was a large four-legged wooden table where the family ate, gathered, and enjoyed guests and each other's company. For some unknown reason, the burglar took one of the legs of the table along with other possessions as he ransacked the home. The family returned to discover their belongings strewn about in heaps, things turned upside down, and the center of their home—the table—seemingly broken, leaning onto the floor with its fourth leg missing.

They went about their way trying to make the best of the situation after getting over the devastation of the violation and loss. They picked up their things and tried to set the home in order again. They went to their jobs and to school the next day, but the table was askew and there was no place to gather because it kept falling over. Things felt off. They propped it up but the propping didn't last very long. Finally, after several days, the woman took the table to a woodworker and had him rearrange the three remaining legs so that the table could balance. It was the same table, just re-centered with the legs that were left. The table was again useful and once again became the center of the home. It was still a table after all.

This is where we are. Don was that fourth leg that made the table of our lives feel solid. We have had to reshape our "life table" and find a new center, yet we are still a family and still feel the power of his love and his life.

I will always remember his life by his love, good deeds and the way he lived life. In a world without Don LaFontaine, I hope we'll do as he did and said: "Make a mark, not a scar."

LOVE EACH OTHER ANYWAY

My skin is brown
and his is peach
when people stare at us
on the beach
we don't care
we let them stare and

love each other anyway

We said I dos
and made a home
grew more in love
like a classic poem
it's ok to simply say
we love each other anyway

And so we go
along our way
our love is bright
as a sunny day
and as we grow
they'll never know
how we love each other anyway

The heart only sees the other's heart
and is drawn to what it feels
and though outwardly it misconstrues
what skin cannot reveal

That love is love
and pain is pain
the more we love
the more we gain
and why not say
that it's okay
to love each other anyway

—Nita Whitaker LaFontaine

Letters to Don

It is important for me that my children get a chance to voice their truths and to share their experience of the love and the loss of their Dad. These are their unedited words and expressions.

Christine, eldest daughter, 42, speaks:

My earliest memories of my father are of smells.

Strange, but true.

I remember the smell of plastic and chlorine as he slowly pushed me through the pool on my swan raft.

I remember the smells of the subway and the burnt scent of chestnuts in New York City.

He would take me to work to Paramount Studios in Manhattan and I would spend the day pushing the light-up buttons on the oldschool phones pretending to take calls. I would use the film splicer and pretend I was making a movie. I even remember the smell of his secretary's perfume. I'm pretty sure it was White Shoulders.

All of my images of him come in bursts of comfort and warmth. Everything I needed him to be he was. I worshipped him.

His greatness was evident in everything he did. To my father, "mediocrity" was a four-letter word. We didn't have snowmen in front of our house, we had a twenty-foot snow sculpture of King Kong with a perfectly smooth hand big enough for four of us kids to sit in.

No store-bought Halloween costumes for me. No way! One year he spent weeks making me a Headless Horseman costume Tim Burton would have been proud to use in his film. It became legendary in our neighborhood.

My tenth birthday party was a sleepover with an advanced screening of Grease *still un-released in the theaters.*

Then there was the time he brought Ringling Brothers circus to my school . . .

The man didn't just live, he EXUDED. He was a rare greatness.

And now, in retrospect, the most important memories are of sound.

The warm sweetness of his skin against my cheek as I fell asleep listening to the resonance of his voice.

He would whisper to me in the night when I had bad dreams.

He told AMAZING ghost stories.

And later in life, he left outgoing messages on all my friends' answering machines.

I truly believed he would live forever.

Every day, I look into the eyes that my younger son inherited from him and I regret that he will never know his larger than life grandfather. My older son can't remember him, but I will try to be a mother to Riley and Cooper in Dad's honor. For all the disappointment he must have at times felt in me, that would be the most important thing in the world to him.

What I want to relate most about Don is, that despite his stoic reputation, he wore his heart on his sleeve.

And what a heart.

There is no way to put into words how much I revere the father he was, the father he became to my sisters and the husband he was to Nita.

Ironically, it was always what he didn't say that mattered most to me.

And now, his silence is deafening.

Skye, middle daughter, 21, speaks:

Trying to describe what life with my dad was like in a few sentences or paragraphs is impossible, really. The man was too incredible to be summed up in chapters, but I guess we do our best.

You know how teenagers or younger girls say that movies have messed up their chances at finding the perfect guy because they make them so fantastic they feel they have no chance of finding them in the real world? Well forget the movies. My dad was and still is the man I hold all other men up to. No one will ever be able to fill those HUGE shoes of his, no matter how hard they try, but he is the example that was set for me.

He treated mom like a queen and me and Liisi like princesses. He gave us the best life we could have ever asked for. He made my first 18 years so much fun. Traveling around the world seeing the most amazing sites, cracking up at his attempts to dance in our front entryway, the best Sweet 16 a girl could ask for—he made it all look so easy; and he showed me that if you work hard enough and truly love what you do, you can have a life that you are proud of and love every second of.

I am proud to say that I am a daddy's girl. From the time I was really little I would miss preschool just to ride around with him and see how he worked; I thought he was just the coolest. Rolling around with him all day did give me a little warped sense of life, I mean, I thought that everyone rolled up to school in a limo, or got to travel to a new place every summer, or had a menagerie of animals. By the time I got into elementary school I wised up a bit. I realized that dad gave us an extraordinary life.

Normal is not the word used to describe my family or my life. Dad was living the dream, and he made every moment count. And he did it all with a smile on his face. He managed to make even the most mundane thing funny. Trying his best to sing along to Frank Sinatra and forgetting all the words, telling me hysterical jokes he just thought up, or trying to disguise his want to cuss out a horrid driver on the freeway. I always arrived home in hysterics, bursting through the door and falling against some chair gasping for breath and trying to tell mom what he had just said.

At home, he managed to be the silly, loving, caring father and husband, as well as a work-a-holic who sometimes didn't come out of his "hole" for hours and hours on end. He was the silliest man, with the singularly most expressive eyebrows I have ever seen on a person. They could be raised to the top of his head when he found something amusing, knitted together when he watched something or got sad, or roaming all around his forehead when he was thinking really hard. The man never stopped, never had an off moment.

From showing off his dream house to friends, to just sitting on his bed reading, he was fully there. At a moment he would be there for me or my sister if we had a bad dream or fought with Mom (which we tried not to do much 'cause seriously, who wants the voice of God getting mad at them? It's terrifying).

He was a man who would do anything for his family. He wanted me and my sister to have everything he didn't have as a kid, so anything we asked for (within reason, mind you) we got. And he was so devoted to Mom, I really don't think I've ever seen two sillier people who couldn't have been more in love. I really had the definition of weird parents, but they had such an amazing marriage, the only thing they ever fought over was how much salt dad put on his food! They were a perfect yet unconventional match.

Dad lived life to the fullest, and he took us all along for the ride. All he wanted was to make us happy, and by doing that he made himself such a happy man.

When he got sick, I honestly thought nothing of it; he was the strongest man I ever knew, and I thought he would be absolutely fine. For a while, it looked like I was right, apart from him slowing down a bit, you would have never known he was sick. When he took a turn for the worse, I just assumed that like most things, it had to get better before it got worse. He started having to carry around oxygen tanks, and started losing weight. Being the strong man he was, he made jokes about it so we all would feel better, but in the back of my mind I knew that things weren't right.

Our car rides became less frequent, while trips to the hospital seemed to become the new norm. I kept blaming the doctors for everything that was happening to him, and for a while I stayed so mad at them. Seeing him sick in a hospital is a mental image that I will never be able to erase. My strong, silly father, looking weak and sad in his hospital gown.

I remember the last day I saw him so well. Liisi had some stomach bug and was passed out on the floor in his and Mom's closet. I went into the room because Mom said Dad was having some trouble and when I was headed down the hall I heard the sound of the ambulance. It wasn't the first time one had been to the house, but it was still scary to know he had to go back. I stayed by his side while the paramedics came up and put him on a gurney. I wanted to get Liisi up to say goodbye but she was really out of it so I left her there. I ran down the stairs so I could be with Dad when he got down there and headed outside. The last thing I ever actually heard him say was that he needed oxygen because he couldn't breathe. I didn't realize that I had just seen him alive for the last time.

He was in the hospital for 9 days, and because the doctors kept saying that he was getting better, and Mom didn't want us seeing him all hooked up to machines, me and Liisi only visited once. We didn't go into his room, but we did wait with family in the waiting room we practically took over. The day before he passed, the doctors were saying that his outlook was good and that he was such a fighter. Me and Liisi went to a friend's party the next day for some time away from the sadness of the hospital. Towards the end of it Liisi got a text from a cousin that said she was sorry to hear about dad. Red flags went off for me and we headed home.

Mom hadn't called so I thought nothing was really wrong but the second we walked in the house to her standing there with tears in her eyes, I knew that something was really, really wrong. Our family friends were there with a beautiful stained glass unicorn that had been painted for dad, and when I saw them I felt like I was about to pass out. Mom scooped me and Liisi in to her and quietly told us that Dad was gone. I broke down. I started crying so hard my head hurt. I could hear my sister saying "No, no, no, this is a joke, it's not funny," over and over. Mom took us outside to a bench in the backyard and we sat there and held each other and cried and cried.

Nothing felt right anymore. I couldn't believe that I wouldn't come home to him sitting at his computer like he always did, or take any more car rides with him. All I could do was cry till I felt like I had no tears left.

I shut down after that; went off to my room to call my best friends; I needed all the support I could get. People came over to see us and I would hide in my room, but they always found me, and I would break down again. At the time, I didn't see how my life was supposed to go on. All I could think about was how much he was going to miss. My high school graduation, my wedding, my first home, first child. Everything just seemed pointless. My Dad was gone, the one man I had always looked up to and who loved me more than anything else was gone. My mom and sister were all I had left, and we grew closer than ever during those first few weeks. With their help as well as the help of my friends I managed to get myself together and go back to school, finish my senior year, and move on to college.

I remember being so angry, feeling like my Dad had been snatched away from me way too soon, but knowing that he was finally happy and no longer in any pain made it bearable.

Then, a butterfly. A single orange butterfly. It appeared out of the bright blue sky, fluttered around me, then vanished. Instantly I knew that it was a sign from Dad that he was alright and still watching out for me. Since then I have seen quite a few of these butterflies, and I know that he is up there happy. Looking down, and proud of his daughter. I miss him every single day, and some days are harder than others. I know that I will always feel the pain of missing him, but I am so, so grateful for the 18 years I got to spend with the world's most amazing Dad.

Liisi, youngest daughter, 17, speaks:

Having a Dad like Don was like having a best friend, mentor, and angel living in your house all in the same man. Both of my parents are pretty perfect, but I always connected so much with my Dad. He never doubted my sisters or me and had the most amazing unconditional love for all three of us. It's foreign to me when people talk about their own dads who aren't around or they don't have a good relationship with. I honestly feel like I had the best Dad the world has ever known. Being his daughter was an honor and I will never forget all the valuable lessons he taught me.

He was without a doubt the best person I've ever known. I have yet to meet anyone else like him. Every day was something different and exciting . . . he was so funny and so classy. His old school charm was a breath of fresh air, and I learned a lot about the kind of man that I would like to marry because him. He will always be my model. All of my friends saw him as a second father, too. He took interest in anything and everything they were doing and treated them all like his own. He always reminded them that they were always welcome and safe in our home. After he passed, a lot of my friends told me that he was more of a father to them than their own dads were, and I just realized how lucky I was to have him as my Dad. He loved me so much.

I remember always asking my mom to take me to get new Barbies, and of course she would say I had way too many already and refuse. Then I would go to plan B and head on down to good ole Dad, who would quickly grab his wallet and within two minutes we were on our way to Toys R Us. Being Don LaFontaine's daughter was like Christmas every day. I honestly can't remember a time when I didn't love him even when I was starting to go through my moody teenage years.

It was more than having a Dad. It was having someone to look up to and admire. He was like my best friend. Everyone tells me I get my sense of humor from him, especially my quick wit. I agree. When I was younger, I could never imagine a world without my Dad. He was like a god to me, and now he's actually an angel looking over me all the time. I thought he was invincible. It was shocking and painful and unexpected when we lost him. I didn't understand how something so bad could happen to someone so amazing who put everyone before himself.

I didn't understand how God could take someone who was so needed and loved. I was only fourteen when he passed, and although it's almost three years later, and I am now seventeen the wound is yet to heal. They say it gets easier with time, but I know that at least twice a week if not more I still to this day have dreams about him still being alive. I would give anything for him to come back just for a few more days so I can tell him and show him how much I love him. But time moves forward and I need to realize that that is not possible.

My mom has allowed my sister and I to understand that it never gets easier, but you learn to live with it. Life does go on and I can say that I honestly am truly happy again although there is a part of me still hurting. I truly admire my family for how well we have started to heal.

My mom is a saint and the best woman I know, and she has stayed so strong through this whole process. My sister Skye and I both talk about him all the time and everything we do we do in dedication to him and my mommy. In my opinion they are both people who the world should know and respect. I just hope that when I grow up, I can be as successful, loving and wonderful as both of my parents, and hope I can live up to the LaFontaine name. Yes, I could never imagine a world without my dad, but now I'm living in it. It's scary and sad sometimes but I feel his warmth and love all around me. I know that everything happens for a reason, and because of him I know who I want to be and what I want to do with my life. I hope and pray that I make him and my mom proud every day and I try to be the best person I can be because of both of them.

Daddy, I love you more than you will ever know, and more than I ever got the chance to say. There are so many things I wish I could tell you, but I know you are having fun up there with George Washington, Gandhi, and Grandma. I miss you every single day, but I'm getting better. I have so many things to thank you for, but most of all I just want to thank you for being my dad, because you made me the luckiest girl in the world.

Sleep tight<3

I, Nita, wife of Don, Mother to Skye and Liisi, speak:

August 26, 2010, is the seventieth anniversary of the day Don LaFontaine came to this world. It's hard to think of 70 and Don in the same sentence because his spirit, life-force, and largess never matched with the age given him. He was so much younger and so much more . . . And because the magnitude of your love, your kind spirit, and how your voice touched us all so deeply and left an indelible loveprint on our hearts forever, we celebrate you and speak your name. For being there for so many in their time of need with a tireless generosity and an open heart, we celebrate you Don. You taught us all to live larger, laugh harder, be a better friend than is expected, and to reach for our biggest dreams, for that we celebrate you. The movies trailers and TV spots you lent your voice to make us go to see many more because you drew us into those stories with your piercing, well-dictioned tones and perfect enunciation of your one take reads, we celebrate you Don. For showing your daughters what a loving Dad looks and feels like, and how he shows up, and as Skye said, for raising the bar so high; and for the wisdom they gained simply by being born to your genes, we celebrate you Don and speak your name and we thank God for you.

For the way you made us all want to be better people and grander stewards of random acts of kindness, today we speak your name, tell a Don story to someone, and celebrate you. For the time that our lives collided and turned into a beautiful symphony; and for the way you loved me with abandon and how you made my moments momentous and our years wonder years, I thank you, celebrate you, speak your name, and wear your love like a lovely mink coat on the coldest day . . . proud to show it off and to snuggle in, I celebrate you my love. We all have our stories that we will forever tell, the laughter and joy that still connects us all to you, and the love that you gave individually to us all that has been a life growing elixir, we celebrate you Don LaFontaine and will always speak your name.

Letter from Don

What follows is a letter Don wrote to his former mother-in-law during the last months of her life. His beliefs and vision were so clear, so comforting and lovely. I include this here because these words are Don's—he tells us, in his voice, what so many of us need to hear. The thoughts and convictions he shares in this letter are priceless guidance that anyone on any journey will benefit from encountering.

October 9, 1996

Dear Mom,

All I can say is I truly believe that this is not all there is. I believe that a great and wondrous adventure lies ahead for all of us, and a lifespan is only the prologue. I believe what awaits us is beyond human imagination and comprehension—and that's what makes it terrifying and compelling.

I believe that the time of paying dues ends—and the time of collecting the rewards begins—and little that we do, good or bad, has anything to do with the outcome.

And I believe that peace and comfort are out there—and well worth the journey.

As for the rest—the past—I prefer to remember the good times, the happy times—because they are the only times that count. I much prefer to remember them, and you, with love and affection.

Nita and I are praying for you. Each road ends in its own time. Nobody is ever gone, only gone ahead. Lead on, Mom, and wait for us.

God bless you, now and forever,

Don

Family Album

Don, age 17

Family picture, Deer Valley, 1997

Don, age 7

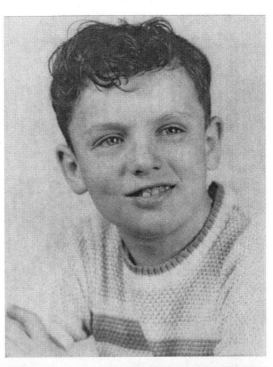

Christine, Skye, Liisi, Riley (eldest grandson, age 3, right) and Cooper (youngest grandson, age 1)

3 Generations: Don, baby Riley, and Christine

Early family portrait. From left, Don, Kathy Scott, JeRelle (her daughter), Jamar (her son), Pappa Green, Alene (oldest sister), Jr., Nita and baby Skye, LaVernon (Alene's son) down front

Mom Ola Mae and Dad Green Whitaker Sr. (at Alene's wedding, 1973)

Our wedding day: from left Alene, Nita, Jr., Kathy, Daddy Green

Don working with
Orson Wells

Don, The Godfather
of the movie trailers

Don as a boy, around age 4, with his sister Sandra, age 2
(look how he is holding her hand)

Wedding Day, Nita and Don, October 1, 1988 Four Seasons Hotel

Don (he quit smoking and plumped up a bit) and dear friend Paul Pape

Christmas card picture 2001, Liisi (with dog Jack), Don, Skye, Christine, and me (and note Retriever Roseanne swimming in the pool!)

Liisi, age 17

2008 at Christine's wedding in PA: Liisi, Chrissy, and Skye

Me and Ben Vereen

Me and Don at home

Little Liisi, around 18 months

Liisi wearing a Diana Ross wig!

Don shopping in small village Eze, southern France

Skye, age 18, high school graduation picture

Ho Ho Ho
The LaFontaines 2011

Christmas 2011, the LaFontaine girls go glam!

Me and Don, 1989, at "I Love my Husband" birthday bash

Skye's Sweet 16 and Liisi age 12

Don, Rubie (Don's mom), and Uncle Zack Whitaker (paternal uncle)—all ascended—at Don's 60th birthday bash

Mamma Nita with my girls singing together . . .
just one of the many times we do!

Skye, age 8, and Liisi, age 4, Christmas card, 1998

Don and me loving on each other

Christmas card, caption read, "We hope your holidays
are as beautiful as we are" ... an inspired Don tag

Liisi inside giant bubble, holding Jack

Liisi and Daddy

Don and me ready for a '70s party!

Me with our doggies
Dutchess and Jack

My favorite picture of us

Liisi's 8th grade graduation with Maria (housekeeper of 13 years) and her Pappa Green

Dad's house in Louisiana, Pappa Green and his children

Me, Skye, and Liisi in Hawaii, 2009

Girls jumping in the Hawaii sun

Grandma Rubie with Sandra's five sons, our nephews
(left to right, top row) Jason, Chad, Shane
(bottom row, left to right) Galen, Rubie, Corey

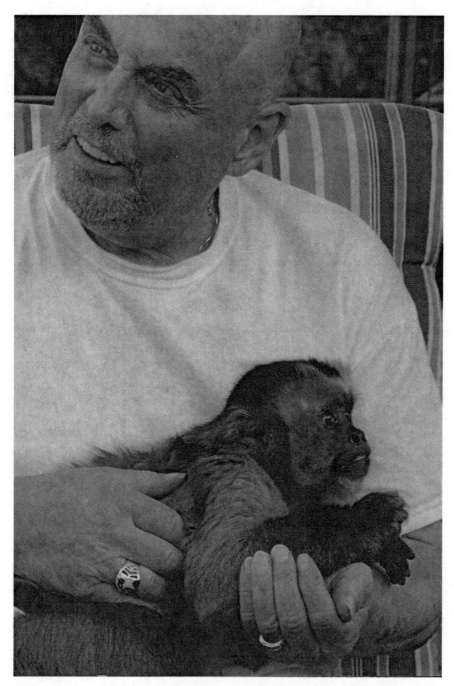

Don with a monkey we had at the house for Skye's 18th; they fell in love

Don with his daughters

Me singing in a Louisiana Pageant, gettin' down!

Skye and Liisi, ages 2 and 6

A sweet moment on our wedding day

The real Don and Nita (better known as LeRoi and Loretta!)

Wedding party October 1, 1988 (yep we did it big!)

Don on set working for Paramount Pictures

Don with Clint Eastwood on the set of **Return to Alcatrez**

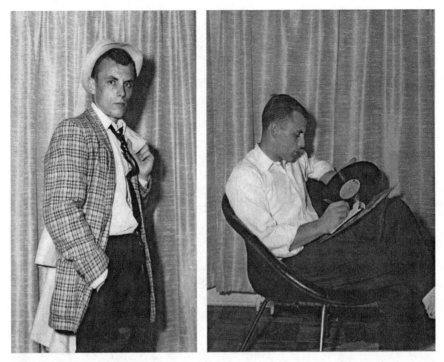

Don, age 20 (approx.), very James Dean   *Don, age 21, working*

Close up of Don's hands as he autographs **Secrets of Voice-Over Success,** *a book he wrote a chapter for*

Don in Alaska on a glacier (Flying helicopters was one of his favorite hobbies)

Skye and Liisi in adventure mode

Don pretending to pee in an Alaskan glacier that he thought looked like a butt crack! Classic Don!

Don and me on a cruise ship in 2002

Don in the army,
age 18 or 19.
SO HANDSOME!

My boy and Adam Jackson

Liisi and Nana

Dutchess, one of our four dogs

Skye and Grandma Rubie (or Nana as they called her)

Nita speaking about Don at The Voiceover Conference, 2010

Nita model shot

Mommy, Skye, and Liisi
at Highland Hall
pentathalon games

Skye and Liisi
at the zoo

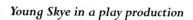
Young Skye in a play production

Daddy and Skye, age 4

Don hogging poker chips

*Best friend Steve Susskind, Don, Ted Lange, and Loren Dryfuss
(poker pals for years) at Ted Lange's wedding*

*In Hawaii, 1994, with Don holding a large bird, Skye, baby Liisi at 3 months
and niece JeRelle*

*Playground with Skye and Liisi
and friend's dog*

*Mamma Rubie at 1988
wedding rehearsal*

Nana and little Liisi

Baby Skye's first bikini
age 11 months

Sisters with smiles and new teeth

Pappa Green and chubby Skye

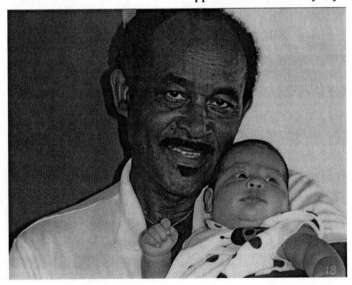

Our family in our favorite place, Hawaii

The girls and their Dad getting a favorite treat

Angel on the Beach *by James Freeheart, the artist we met on the beach in Hawaii*

CPSIA information can be obtained
at www.ICGtesting.com
Printed in the USA
FSOW01n2154091117
40991FS